D1631157

THE IRISH GRANNY'S
POCKET
RECIPE
BOOK

LEABHARLANN
CO. CILL DARA

OVER 110 CLASSIC DISHES

Gill & Macmillan
Hume Avenue, Park West, Dublin 12

www.gillmacmillanbooks.ie

Copyright © Teapot Press Ltd 2013

ISBN: 978-0-7171-5900-0

This book was created and produced by Teapot Press Ltd

Written & Edited by Fiona Biggs
Designed by Tony Potter & Ginny Zeal
Picture research and additional photography by Ben Potter
Home economics by Ben Potter & Imogen Tyler

Printed in PRC

This book is typeset in Garamond and Dax

A CIP catalogue record for this book is available
from the British Library.

5 4 3 2

THE IRISH GRANNY'S
POCKET
RECIPE
BOOK

Contents

Contents

Introduction

Think of traditional Irish food and you'll probably come up with Irish Stew, Dublin Coddle, Bacon & Cabbage (or Corned Beef & Cabbage, which is not even a traditional Irish dish, simply an example of Irish emigrants to the United States making the best of available ingredients) and, of course, potatoes!

However, the story of Irish food is much richer and more varied than these stereotypes. It's all about food in season, simply cooked, making ingenious use of very limited cooking facilities. To augment the basic diet, foodstuffs were foraged from the fields, hedgerows and even the seashore – mushrooms, berries, rosehips, nuts, crab apples, seaweed, mussels, crabs and limpets were just a few of the ingredients brought home to the cook. Even very unlikely ingredients – nettles, thistles and dandelions – were used. Most rural households kept a few hens, so eggs were plentiful and were often bartered for staples such as flour and sugar. Milk and butter were readily available, as were their many by-products, such as curds and buttermilk.

Nothing was wasted – many families would have kept a pig, whose meat was cured and salted and eaten during the long winter months. It's sometimes said that the Irish used to eat every part of the pig except its grunt! However, it is true that every bit of the pig was used, including the stomach, intestines and even the trotters, which provided that prized delicacy, crubeens. The blood was used to make a type of blood sausage known as black pudding, which is a staple of the traditional Irish cooked breakfast.

Fresh vegetables were eaten in season because there were few methods of preservation available – what Irish child of the last century doesn't have a memory of sitting at the kitchen table shelling a big bowl of fresh peas? Root vegetables and other humble crops grow well in Ireland and have an important role in our cooking, even though they might be disparaged in other parts of the world. Berries and other fruit, such as apples, were often stewed and served as a simple dessert with custard, or made into pies, jams and jellies.

Apart from pork, meat was rarely eaten, reserved for special occasions. Chicken was a Sunday luxury, and people would try to have a goose at Christmas. For those living on the coast fish was plentiful and readily available, but it began to be seen as a penitential food when the Catholic Church banned meat on Fridays. Over-fishing has made fish less available, more expensive and, paradoxically, more desirable. Freshwater fish, including the wonderful wild salmon, were once-a-year treats, if you were lucky.

Irish cooking was, of course, influenced by the cuisine of the various settlers in the country over a period of 800 years.

The Normans brought a French influence, with an emphasis on the use of herbs and spices and a tradition of using dried fruits, such as raisins and dates.

The potato was introduced in the seventeenth century, and was so well adapted to the Irish soil that it soon became a staple food, which led to the disaster of famine in the nineteenth century when blight caused the potato crop to fail. Nevertheless, it is still a favourite food, cooked in many different ways – with lots of recipes for using up leftover potatoes as well.

In the eighteenth and nineteenth centuries the kitchens of the landed gentry produced food cooked in ways never before encountered in Ireland. Some of these cooking methods were introduced to ordinary people by family members serving in the big houses and adapted to suit the cooking equipment available to them. Most dishes were cooked in a bastible, a lidded iron pot that was hung over an open fire. Irish cooks were adept in the use of this pot, preparing a wide range of dishes, from stews to soda bread to upside-down fruit cakes!

Wheat flour was a luxury, and oats, which are particularly well adapted to the damp Irish climate and soil conditions, were frequently used in a range of dishes, like porridge, soups and sweetened and unsweetened biscuits. Cakes needed expensive ingredients and were rare, usually reserved for special occasions. They were not fancy pastries but good, solid offerings, utilizing what might be to hand – dried fruit, home-made jam, a little alcohol, cold tea.

No account of Irish food would be complete without mentioning stout. Regarded not just as an alcoholic drink, but almost as a foodstuff, it was even recommended to mothers-to-be as a good source of iron. In the kitchen, it found its way into stews, cakes and desserts.

In the 1960s and 1970s a different attitude to food became noticeable. More and more people moved to cities for work and convenience foods in cans and packets became fashionable. Home-made meals made with fresh ingredients became increasingly less socially acceptable than anything bought in a shop. Domestic science and home economics classes in school were sidelined in favour of more 'useful' subjects, and a generation of Irish people grew up without any real idea of how to cook.

Things now seem to have come full circle, and although an enormous variety of ready meals is now available, there is also a growing interest in cooking from scratch using good, fresh ingredients. Irish people are cooking with confidence, adapting traditional recipes to include influences from abroad. Sometimes, however, only the original recipe will do to give you the sense of comfort and warmth you experienced when you sat in your granny's kitchen.

BREAKFASTS

There's nothing quite like a good breakfast to set you up for the day. This selection of Granny's favourites has something for everyone, whether you're relaxing on a lazy Sunday morning or in a hurry to get to work.

Is maith an pósadh, ach is é an bricfeasta le chéile go n-eascraíonn an trioblóid go léir.

Marriages are all happy.
It's having breakfast together that causes all the trouble.

Irish Saying

INGREDIENTS

140 g/5 oz pinhead oatmeal

850 ml/1½ pints water

pinch of salt

fresh or stewed fruit, cream or brown sugar, to serve

accompaniment of your choice according to taste and season

Porridge

Porridge is usually made with rolled oats, which cook in 10 minutes. However, made the old-fashioned way with pinhead oatmeal, soaked overnight, the porridge will have a lovely nutty texture.

METHOD

Put the oatmeal into a saucepan with the water and leave to stand in a cool place overnight.

Add the salt and bring to the boil over a medium heat, stirring frequently. Reduce the heat and simmer for 20 minutes until thickened.

Serve immediately with your choice of accompaniment.

SERVES 4

1 tomato, halved
vegetable oil, for
drizzling and frying
2 pork sausages
2 back bacon rashers
2 slices white
pudding
2 slices black
pudding
mushrooms
1 large egg
salt and freshly
ground black pepper
fresh white soda
bread (page 182),
to serve

Full Irish Breakfast

Served today as a staple in Ireland's many
wonderful bed and breakfasts, it used to
be reserved for Sundays and feastdays.

METHOD

Drizzle the tomato halves with oil and season with salt and
pepper. Place the sausages on a rack under a hot grill and cook,
turning once, for about 15 minutes, until browned all over. Add
the tomatoes during the last 4 minutes of cooking.

Meanwhile, put the rashers into a dry frying pan over a high
heat and fry for 3 minutes on each side, or until cooked to your
liking.

Remove from the pan using a slotted spoon, drain on kitchen
paper and keep warm.

Add the pudding slices to the pan, fry for 1–2 minutes on each
side, then remove from the pan, drain on kitchen paper and
keep warm. Use the same pan to fry a sliced mushroom.

Heat some oil in a separate small frying pan, carefully break in
the egg and fry over a low heat until cooked to your liking.

Transfer all the cooked ingredients to a warmed plate and serve
with plenty of soda bread.

SERVES 1

INGREDIENTS

3 eggs
125 ml/4 fl oz milk
1 tsp vanilla extract
pinch of ground
nutmeg
6 slices of day-old
white bread
butter, for frying
fresh berries,
preserves, whipped
cream, maple syrup,
icing sugar or caster
sugar, to serve

French Toast

A delicious way to make a few eggs go a
long way, French toast can be as indulgent
or as healthy as you like, depending on
what you serve it with.

METHOD

Beat the eggs with the milk in a large, wide bowl. Add the
vanilla extract and nutmeg and stir to combine.

Melt some butter in a wide frying pan over a medium heat.

Meanwhile, soak the bread slices in the egg mixture, allowing
any excess to drip off. Place the bread in the pan in batches and
fry for 4–5 minutes on each side until golden. Keep the cooked
bread warm until ready to serve.

Serve hot with your choice of accompaniment.

SERVES 4

Scrambled Eggs with Smoked Salmon

INGREDIENTS

8 large eggs
2 tbsp single cream
55 g/2 oz butter
125 g/4 oz smoked salmon trimmings
salt and freshly ground black pepper
chopped fresh flatleaf parsley, to garnish
wholemeal toast, to serve

This luxurious breakfast or brunch dish is quite economical as you can use those little supermarket packs of smoked salmon trimmings. If you have some trimmings from a whole side of smoked salmon, so much the better!

METHOD

Beat the eggs with the cream in a large bowl and season to taste with salt and pepper.

Melt the butter in a frying pan over a medium heat. Add the eggs to the pan and cook, stirring occasionally, for about 3 minutes, until just cooked.

Remove the pan from the heat, fold in the smoked salmon and transfer to warmed plates.

Garnish with parsley and serve immediately, with toast.

SERVES 4

GRANNY'S TIP: Add the salt just before cooking, to prevent the eggs from becoming rubbery.

INGREDIENTS

butter, for greasing
4 large eggs
salt and buttered
toast fingers, to
serve

Coddled Eggs

Coddled eggs are a cross between boiled eggs and poached eggs. They can be cooked and served in the same cup and are very popular with young children as dippers for toast 'soldiers'.

METHOD

Grease 4 heatproof cups or egg coddlers. Break 1 egg into each cup, then place the cups in a wide saucepan. Add boiling water to the pan to a depth of 2.5 cm/1 inch, then cover and cook for 3–4 minutes, depending on how you like your eggs.

Remove from the heat and serve immediately with salt and buttered toast fingers.

SERVES 4

SOUPS & STARTERS

Don't save these for a three-course dinner, but follow Granny's example and have these delicious one-dish meals for lunch or supper instead.

Tús maith, leath na hoibre.
A good start is half of the work.

Irish Saying

INGREDIENTS

2 tbsp butter

850 ml/1½ pints
fresh vegetable stock
or chicken stock

700 ml/1¼ pints
milk

3 tbsp rolled oats

6 large leeks,
trimmed and sliced
into 2.5-cm/1-inch
chunks

salt and freshly
ground black pepper

1 tbsp chopped fresh
parsley

150 ml/5 fl oz single
cream, to garnish

SERVES 4

Brotchán

A delicious hearty soup for a cold winter's day that is both economical and filling.

METHOD

Put the butter, stock and milk into a large saucepan over a medium heat and bring to the boil.

Add the oats, bring back to the boil and cook for 5 minutes, then add the leeks and season to taste with salt and pepper. Cover, reduce the heat and simmer for 30 minutes.

Add the parsley and cook for a further 5 minutes. Transfer to warmed bowls, add a swirl of cream to each and serve immediately.

INGREDIENTS

25 g/1 oz butter

450 g/1 lb parsnips, peeled and sliced

1 Bramley apple, peeled and chopped

1.2 litres/2 pints vegetable stock

½ tsp dried sage

2 cloves

fresh parsley sprigs, to garnish

Parsnip & Apple Soup

A deliciously creamy yet fresh-tasting soup, which blends two unlikely ingredients.

METHOD

Melt the butter in a large saucepan, then add the parsnips and apple. Cover and cook over a low heat for 10 minutes.

Add the stock, sage and cloves and simmer until the parsnip is softened. Remove and discard the cloves, then pour the contents of the pan into a blender and blend until smooth.

Pour the soup into warmed bowls, garnish with parsley and serve immediately.

SERVES 4

INGREDIENTS

knob of butter

6 potatoes, peeled and diced

2 onions, finely chopped

1.5 litres/2¾ pints fresh vegetable stock

salt and freshly ground black pepper

chopped fresh parsley, to garnish

Potato Soup

A very simple and heartwarming soup, the ultimate in winter comfort food.

METHOD

Melt the butter in a large saucepan over a medium heat, then add the potatoes and onions and cook for about 10 minutes until the onions are translucent.

Add the stock and season with salt and plenty of pepper. Reduce the heat and simmer for about 30 minutes.

Pass the soup through a sieve, then return to the pan and reheat.

Pour the soup into warmed bowls, garnish with parsley and serve immediately.

SERVES 6

Nettle Soup

A traditional spring soup, made with young nettle leaves – bursting with fresh flavour and full of essential iron.

INGREDIENTS

3 tbsp butter
500 g/1 lb 2 oz potatoes, peeled and cut into chunks
1 small onion, thinly sliced
1 small leek, thickly sliced
1 litre/1¾ pints fresh vegetable stock
175 g/6 oz fresh young nettle leaves, finely chopped
150 ml/5 fl oz milk
salt and freshly ground black pepper
cream to decorate

METHOD

Melt the butter in a heavy saucepan, then add the potatoes, onion and leek and toss to coat. Add salt and pepper to taste, cover and cook over a low heat for about 10 minutes.

Add the stock, bring to the boil over a medium heat, then reduce the heat and simmer for 10 minutes.

Add the nettle leaves and cook very briefly. Add the milk and stir, then pour into a blender and liquidize.

Return to the pan and heat, then season to taste and serve in warmed bowls with a dash of cream.

SERVES 6

GRANNY'S TIP: Take care not to overcook the nettles as they will lose their lovely flavour.

INGREDIENTS

600 ml/1 pint water
1 bay leaf
juice of 1 lemon
550 g/1 lb 4 oz
undyed smoked
haddock, cut into
large chunks
2 tbsp butter
1 small onion, finely
chopped
225 g/8 oz small or
button mushrooms,
sliced
1 tbsp plain flour
425 ml/15 fl oz hot
milk
freshly ground black
pepper
grated lemon rind
and chopped fresh
parsley, to garnish

Smoked Haddock & Mushroom Soup

This richly flavoured soup, based on milk rather than stock, is full of wholesome goodness.

METHOD

Bring the water to the boil in a large saucepan, then add the bay leaf and a little of the lemon juice. Add the fish, season to taste with pepper and poach for 5 minutes.

Transfer the fish to a plate and set aside, reserving the poaching liquid.

Melt the butter in a separate large saucepan, add the onion and mushrooms and sauté until softened. Add the flour and mix well to combine.

Gradually add the milk and the reserved liquid, stirring constantly until the desired consistency is achieved.

Return the fish to the soup and reheat over a low heat.

Pour into warmed bowls, garnish with lemon rind and parsley and serve immediately.

GRANNY'S TIP: If you use smoked haddock, it is quite salty, so resist the temptation to add more salt to the soup.

SERVES 6

Mutton Broth

A substantial old-fashioned soup, often served as a one-course meal rather than as a starter.

INGREDIENTS

450 g/1 lb lean neck of lamb, diced

280 g/10 oz carrots, diced

175 g/6 oz onions, diced

2 leeks, sliced

1 white turnip, diced

2 tbsp pearl barley

1.7 litres/3 pints water

salt and freshly ground black pepper

finely chopped fresh parsley, to garnish

METHOD

Put the meat, carrots, onions, leeks, turnip and barley into a large saucepan. Season to taste with plenty of salt and pepper and add the water.

Cover and bring to the boil over a medium heat, then reduce the heat and simmer for 1½–2 hours.

Pour into warmed bowls, garnish with parsley and serve immediately.

SERVES 6

INGREDIENTS

10 potatoes, peeled
and cut into cubes

5 leeks, trimmed
and thinly sliced

4-6 tbsp milk

1.5 litres/2½ pints
water

salt and freshly
ground black pepper

croûtons and single
cream, to garnish

Leek & Potato Soup

A delicious, mild-flavoured lunchtime
soup, best served with lots of fresh crusty
bread and butter.

METHOD

Put the potatoes and leeks into a large saucepan of lightly salted
water, bring to the boil and cook for 15–20 minutes, or until
tender.

Remove from the heat, take out some leeks and potatoes using
a slotted spoon and reserve to garnish. Transfer the remaining
vegetables and the cooking liquid to a blender and blend until
smooth. Return to the pan and add salt and pepper to taste. Stir
in the milk and heat until hot.

Serve in warmed bowls, garnished with the reserved vegetables,
croûtons and a swirl of cream.

SERVES 8

*GRANNY'S TIP: For a richer finish, replace the milk with an equal
quantity of single cream.*

INGREDIENTS

2 tbsp olive oil
2 onions, chopped
2 tbsp plain flour
1.2 litres/2 pints
vegetable stock
fresh crusty bread,
to serve

Onion Soup

A simple yet healthy soup that will warm you up on a cold winter's evening and help keep colds and flu at bay.

METHOD

Heat the oil in a large saucepan, add the onions and fry until softened. Add the flour and stock and mix to combine. Cook over a low heat for 30 minutes.

Serve in warmed bowls with crusty bread.

SERVES 6

INGREDIENTS

2 tbsp vegetable oil
600 g/1 lb 5 oz beef kidney, skinned, cored and sliced
2 tbsp flour
2 litres/3½ pints beef stock
1 tbsp sugar
1 sachet bouquet garni
1 tsp fresh lemon juice
125 ml/4 fl oz medium sherry
salt and freshly ground black pepper

Irish Kidney Soup

A hearty, beefy soup with tons of rich flavour and an unexpected citrussy zing.

METHOD

Heat the oil in a large saucepan, then add the meat and cook, turning occasionally, until browned all over. Drain the excess fat, then stir in the flour and cook for 1 minute.

Add the stock, sugar and bouquet garni. Bring to the boil, then reduce the heat, cover and simmer for about 3 hours.

Leave to cool, then chill in the refrigerator for 1 hour. Remove and discard the bouquet garni and skim the fat from the surface of the soup.

Season to taste, add the lemon juice and sherry and liquidize in a blender. Transfer to a clean saucepan, heat until piping hot and serve in warmed bowls.

SERVES 6

Pea Soup

This recipe uses dried marrowfat peas, a traditional accompaniment to the Sunday roast. They require soaking overnight with a little bicarbonate of soda, which give the peas a unique flavour.

INGREDIENTS

1 tbsp vegetable oil
1 onion, chopped
2 celery sticks, chopped
1 garlic clove, peeled and crushed
1.2 litres/2 pints water
225 g/8 oz dried marrowfat peas, soaked in water overnight and drained
1 sachet bouquet garni

METHOD

Heat the oil in a large saucepan, add the onion and cook over a medium heat until browned. Add the celery and garlic and cook for about 5 minutes.

Add the water, peas and bouquet garni, bring to the boil, then reduce the heat and simmer for about 2½ hours. Remove from the heat, then remove and discard the bouquet garni.

Transfer the soup to a blender and blend until smooth. Transfer to a clean saucepan and heat until piping hot, then serve immediately in warmed bowls.

SERVES 8

Creamy Oyster Bisque

A rich and luxurious soup for a special occasion, traditionally served in pubs at the annual Galway Oyster Festival, which takes place in September.

INGREDIENTS

225 ml/8 fl oz fresh fish stock
1 small white onion, diced
1 celery stalk, diced
125 ml/4 fl oz Irish stout
450 g/1 lb potatoes, peeled and diced
1 tsp fresh thyme
24 fresh oysters, carefully removed from their shells
125 ml/4 fl oz milk
freshly ground black pepper
chopped fresh watercress or parsley, to garnish

METHOD

Heat 2 tablespoons of the stock in a large saucepan. Add the onion and celery and cook over a medium heat until translucent. Add the stout, remaining stock, potatoes and thyme, bring to the boil and cook until the potatoes are softened.

Transfer to a blender, add half the oysters, the milk, and pepper to taste and blend until smooth.

Return to the pan and bring to the boil, then serve immediately in warmed bowls, garnished with the remaining oysters and some watercress.

SERVES 4–6

INGREDIENTS

55 g/2 oz butter
225 g/8 oz potatoes,
peeled and diced
115 g/4 oz button
mushrooms, sliced
1 onion, sliced
450 g/1 lb spinach,
rinsed and chopped
1 litre/1¾ pints
chicken stock
¼ tsp ground cloves
115 g/4 oz rolled
oats
salt and freshly
ground black pepper
fennel fronds, to
garnish

Spinach & Mushroom Soup

This delicious vegetable soup is thickened with oatmeal and spiced with cloves, giving it an interesting texture and flavour.

METHOD

Melt the butter in a large saucepan over a low heat. Add the potatoes, mushrooms and onion and fry until softened.

Add the spinach, stock and cloves and season to taste with salt and pepper.

Stir in the oats, bring to the boil, then reduce the heat and simmer for about 20 minutes. Transfer to a blender and blend until smooth.

Garnish with fennel fronds and serve hot in warmed bowls.

GRANNY'S TIP: If you don't like cloves, replace them with an equal quantity of ground nutmeg.

SERVES 4

Irish Eggs

This can be served as a light lunch dish, but it also makes a delicious starter for hungry diners.

INGREDIENTS

500 g/1 lb 2 oz mashed potatoes

4 hardboiled eggs, chopped

3 spring onions, trimmed and chopped

115 g/4 oz mature Cheddar cheese, grated

pinch of English mustard powder

2 tbsp seasoned flour

1 egg, beaten

3 tbsp dried golden breadcrumbs

vegetable oil, for deep-frying

shredded lettuce and cherry tomato quarters, to serve

METHOD

Mix the potatoes, hard-boiled eggs, spring onions, cheese and mustard together and season to taste with salt and pepper.

Divide the mixture into 8 portions and roll each portion into a ball.

Roll the balls in the seasoned flour, dip in the beaten egg, then roll in the breadcrumbs until coated.

Meanwhile, heat enough oil for deep-frying in a large saucepan or deep-fat fryer to 180°C/350°F, or until a cube of bread turns golden and crisp in 30 seconds.

Add the balls to the oil and fry for 10–12 minutes until golden brown.

Serve on a bed of lettuce with cherry tomato quarters.

SERVES 4

Dublin Bay Prawns

Otherwise known as langoustines, these delicious crustaceans are best cooked and served with their shells on.

INGREDIENTS

1 kg/2 lb 4 oz
Dublin Bay Prawns,
shell on

2 onions, thinly
sliced

300 ml/10 fl oz
olive oil

1 tbsp brandy

1 chicken stock cube

200 ml/7 fl oz water

1 tsp sugar

2 tbsp finely
chopped fresh
parsley

salt and freshly
ground black pepper

METHOD

Remove the legs and whiskers from the prawns and wash the shellfish under cold running water.

Put the onions into a colander and pour over a little boiling water.

Heat the oil in a large saucepan, add the onions and sauté until translucent. Add the prawns and sauté, then add the brandy.

Crumble in the stock cube, then add the water, sugar and parsley and season to taste. Bring to the boil, then simmer for 2–3 minutes.

Serve immediately in warmed bowls.

SERVES 6

Smoked Salmon Pâté

This simple Irish starter is traditionally served with fresh brown soda bread, but it is also delicious with a toasted baguette.

INGREDIENTS

125 g/4 oz smoked salmon trimmings

200 g/7 oz canned red salmon

125 g/4 ½ oz cream cheese

capers and chopped fresh dill, to garnish

toasted baguette slices or brown soda bread (page 184), to serve

METHOD

Put the smoked salmon, canned salmon, cream cheese and butter into a food processor and process until smooth.

Pack the mixture into 4 ramekins, smoothing the surface, then cover with clingfilm and chill for at least 2–3 hours.

Garnish with capers and dill and serve with toast.

SERVES 4

INGREDIENTS

24 fresh oysters
shredded lettuce
and crushed ice, to
garnish
lemon slices, to
serve

Fresh Oysters

Something of an acquired taste, these can quickly become addictive, especially if washed down with a glass of stout.

METHOD

Wash the oysters, discarding any that are slightly open. Open the oysters using an oyster knife, reserving any shell juices.

Arrange the lettuce and crushed ice on chilled plates and place the oysters on top, in their shells. Drizzle over the reserved juices.

Serve immediately with lemon slices.

SERVES 4

GRANNY'S TIP: Wrap the hand holding the oyster in a clean tea towel in case the knife slips while you're working.

INGREDIENTS

20 raw Dublin Bay prawns, peeled and deveined

30 g/1 oz plain flour

pinch of cayenne pepper

85 g/3 oz fresh white breadcrumbs

1 large egg, beaten

salt and freshly ground black pepper

lemon wedges and tartare sauce, to serve

Scampi

This starter harks back to the 1970s, when it was served in almost every Irish hotel and restaurant.

METHOD

Rinse the prawns and pat dry with kitchen paper. Line a plate with baking paper.

Put the flour into a bowl, add the cayenne pepper and season to taste with salt and pepper. Spread the breadcrumbs on a wide plate.

Roll each prawn in the flour mixture, then dip in the beaten egg and roll in the breadcrumbs to coat. Transfer to the prepared plate.

Heat the oil in a large, high-sided frying pan to 180°C/350°F, or until a cube of bread turns golden and crisp in 30 seconds.

Add the scampi to the oil in batches and cook for 3 minutes, turning occasionally. Remove with a slotted spoon and drain on kitchen paper.

Serve immediately with lemon wedges and tartare sauce.

SERVES 4

GRANNY'S TIP: To avoid soggy batter, bring the oil back to the correct temperature between batches.

Stuffed Mussels

This is an Irish spin on the French dish of mussels steamed in wine – stout is an excellent partner for shellfish.

INGREDIENTS

48 large mussels

300 ml/10 fl oz Irish stout

225 g/8 oz butter, at room temperature

10 garlic cloves, crushed

110 g/3½ oz fresh white breadcrumbs

2 tbsp chopped fresh parsley

lemon wedges and fresh crusty bread, to serve

SERVES 4–6

METHOD

Clean the mussels under cold running water and pull off the beards, discarding any mussels that are open or that refuse to close when tapped.

Put the mussels into a large saucepan with the stout and a little water and heat until the mussels have opened. Drain the mussels and discard any that remain closed. Remove the top shell of each mussel.

Meanwhile, mix the butter and garlic together, then add the breadcrumbs and parsley and mix to combine. Preheat the grill to high.

Place some of the mixture on each mussel and cook under the hot grill for 5–10 minutes until sizzling.

Serve immediately with lemon wedges and crusty bread.

INGREDIENTS

4 fresh herrings, filleted

1 onion, sliced into rings

1 tsp salt

1 bay leaf

4 cloves

6 white peppercorns

6 black peppercorns

1 tsp sugar

150 ml/5 fl oz Irish stout

150 ml/5 fl oz white malt vinegar

Herrings Potted in Stout

An unusual way to prepare herrings – the liquid makes a lovely jelly if the herrings are chilled overnight.

METHOD

Preheat the oven to 160°C/325°F/Gas Mark 3. Roll up the herring fillets from the tail end and arrange them, seam underneath, in a casserole dish. Top with the onion rings, salt, bay leaf, peppercorns and sugar.

Mix the stout and vinegar together and pour the mixture over the fish. Cover and cook in the preheated oven for 50 minutes, then switch off the oven and leave the casserole in it for 2 hours.

Transfer the fish to a serving dish and spoon over some of the cooking liquid. Chill for at least 2 hours, or overnight.

SERVES 4

INGREDIENTS

55 g/2 oz butter
55 g/2 oz plain flour
150 ml/5 fl oz milk
225 g/8 oz smoked
haddock, cooked and
flaked
225 g/8 oz mashed
potatoes
1 egg, beaten
6 tbsp dried golden
breadcrumbs
vegetable oil, for
frying
salt and freshly
ground black pepper
snipped fresh chives,
to garnish
lemon wedges, to
serve

Smoked Haddock Fishcakes

A substantial starter or a light lunch dish, this is a great way to use up leftover mashed potatoes.

METHOD

Melt the butter in a saucepan over a medium heat, then stir in the flour and cook for 1 minute. Gradually add the milk and cook, stirring constantly, until thickened.

Remove from the heat and leave to cool, then add the fish and potatoes with salt and pepper to taste and mix to combine.

Shape the mixture into 8 round cakes. Dip the cakes in the beaten egg and then in the breadcrumbs, turning to coat.

Heat some oil in frying pan, then add the cakes and fry for 5 minutes on each side until golden brown.

Drain on kitchen paper, garnish with chives and serve immediately with lemon wedges.

SERVES 4

MAIN DISHES

From rib-sticking winter warmers based on meat, to light and delicate summer treats using fresh fish, Granny has a range of dishes to suit every appetite.

Is geall le fleá bia go leor.
Enough food is as good as a feast.

Irish Saying

INGREDIENTS

4 large potatoes, peeled and thickly sliced

450 g/1 lb sausages, each sliced into 4 or 5 pieces

450 g/1 lb streaky bacon rashers, cut into small pieces

2 onions, roughly chopped

300 ml/10 fl oz water

salt and freshly ground black pepper

chopped fresh parsley, to garnish

Dublin Coddle

This hearty winter stew, made with sausages and economical cuts of bacon, is full of flavour.

METHOD

Layer the potatoes, sausages, bacon and onions in a large saucepan, adding salt and pepper to each layer and finishing with a potato layer.

Add the water, then bring to the boil over a medium heat. Reduce the heat and simmer for at least 1 hour.

Serve in warmed bowls, garnished with parsley.

SERVES 4

INGREDIENTS

1 kg/2 lb 4 oz
middle neck of lamb,
trimmed and cut into
chunks
4 large potatoes,
peeled and cut into
chunks
2 carrots, sliced
2 onions, sliced
500 ml/18 fl oz
water
salt and freshly
ground black pepper
fresh parsley sprigs,
to garnish

SERVES 4

Irish Stew

Probably the best known of all traditional Irish dishes, this was originally a white stew made with an economical mutton cut. Nowadays, carrots are often added for colour, and lamb has replaced the mutton.

METHOD

Preheat the oven to 160°C/350°F/Gas Mark 3.

Layer the meat, potatoes, carrots and onions in a casserole dish, adding salt and pepper to each layer and finishing with a layer of potatoes.

Add the water, cover with a tight-fitting lid and cook in the preheated oven for at least 2 hours.

Serve in warmed bowls, garnished with parsley.

INGREDIENTS

vegetable oil, for frying

1 onion, finely chopped

125 g/4 oz streaky bacon rashers, chopped

2 tbsp plain flour

½ tsp mixed herbs

450 g/1 lb lamb's liver, cut into bite-sized pieces

225 ml/8 fl oz lamb stock or beef stock

400 g/14 oz canned chopped tomatoes

1 tbsp Worcestershire sauce

salt and freshly ground black pepper

mashed potatoes and cooked peas, to serve

SERVES 4

Liver & Bacon Casserole

This delicious yet economical dish is a great way of seeing that your family is getting enough iron and zinc.

METHOD

Preheat the oven to 180°C/350°F/Gas Mark 4.

Heat the oil in a frying pan, add the onion and bacon and fry until softened. Remove with a slotted spoon, transfer to a casserole dish and set aside.

Mix the flour and herbs together in a wide dish and season with salt and pepper.

Toss the liver in the seasoned flour until lightly coated, then add to the pan and fry until lightly browned. Transfer to the casserole dish.

Add the stock to the pan and bring to the boil, then stir in the tomatoes. Add the Worcestershire sauce, bring back to the boil, then remove from the heat and add to the casserole dish.

Cover and cook in the preheated oven for 45 minutes.

Serve hot with mashed potatoes and peas.

INGREDIENTS

2 tbsp olive oil

2 bay leaves

1.25 kg/2 lb 12 oz stewing beef, cut into chunks

small onions, or 1 large onion, sliced

1 garlic clove, crushed

2 tbsp seasoned flour

150 ml/5 fl oz Irish stout

225 g/8 oz carrots, thickly sliced

115 g/4 oz button mushrooms, sliced

½ tsp dried mixed herbs

salt and freshly ground black pepper

chopped fresh parsley, to garnish

mashed potatoes, to serve

SERVES 4

Mickey Gill's Beef Braised with Stout

The stout in this casserole cooks down to a rich gravy that is soaked up by creamy mashed potatoes.

METHOD

Preheat the oven to 160°C/325°F/Gas Mark 3.

Heat the oil in a large casserole dish and add the bay leaves. Add the beef and cook, turning frequently, until browned. Remove the beef and set aside.

Add the onion and garlic to the oil and sauté until softened. Return the beef to the casserole, sprinkle with the seasoned flour and cook until browned. Add the stout and enough cold water to cover the meat.

Add the carrots and mushrooms, season to taste with salt and pepper and bring to the boil. Add the herbs and stir, then cover and cook in the preheated oven for 1½ hours, or until the beef is tender, adding more liquid if needed.

Remove the bay leaves and serve in warmed bowls, garnished with parsley and accompanied by mashed potatoes.

INGREDIENTS

4 x 300 g/10½ oz
sirloin steaks, about
3 cm/1¼ inches
thick
85 g/3 oz butter,
diced
½ tsp freshly ground
black pepper
25 g/1 oz mixed
green and pink
peppercorns
salt

Marinade

300 ml/10 fl oz Irish
stout
300 ml/10 fl oz
chicken stock
pinch of fresh thyme
1 tsp Worcestershire
sauce
1 bay leaf
½ tsp freshly ground
black pepper

SERVES 4

Sirloin Steak Marinated in Irish Stout

Prepared with the finest cuts of superb Irish beef, this is a good dish to serve on a special occasion.

METHOD

Mix all the marinade ingredients in a casserole dish. Add the meat. Cover and leave to marinate for 8 hours, turning occasionally.

Remove the steaks from the marinade, pat dry with kitchen paper, sprinkle with the black pepper and set aside.

Heat the marinade in a saucepan over a high heat until the liquid is reduced by half. Skim off any scum that rises to the surface. Strain into a clean saucepan and set aside.

Cook the steaks under a hot grill, to taste, turning once.

Add the peppercorns to the sauce and heat over a low heat, whisking in the butter a piece at a time. Add salt to taste, then serve the steak with a little sauce poured over and the rest served separately.

INGREDIENTS

900 g/2 lb best quality beef steak, cut into small pieces

1 tbsp seasoned flour

85 g/3 oz butter

8 streaky bacon rashers, chopped

5 onions, chopped

2 carrots, thickly sliced

1 tbsp raisins

1 tsp soft light brown sugar

300 ml/10 fl oz Irish stout

450 g/1 lb ready-rolled shortcrust pastry

beaten egg, for glazing

Steak & Stout Pie

Beef and stout blend perfectly in this delicious pie. The crust is broken open to reveal a rich, dark interior.

METHOD

Roll the meat in the seasoned flour. Melt the butter in a frying pan, then add the beef and the bacon and cook, stirring occasionally, until browned.

Transfer the meat to a casserole dish. Add the onions to the pan and fry until golden. Add to the casserole with the carrots, raisins, sugar and stout.

Cover tightly, bring to the boil over a medium heat, then reduce the heat and simmer for about 2 hours until the meat is tender, adding more liquid if needed.

Meanwhile, preheat the oven to 200°C/400°F/Gas Mark 6. Transfer the contents of the casserole dish to a deep pie dish and cover with the pastry, trimming and sealing the edges. Brush with the beaten egg and cook in the preheated oven for 30–35 minutes, until golden brown.

Serve hot.

SERVES 4

INGREDIENTS

1.8 kg/3 lb 8 oz
shoulder of bacon,
soaked in cold water
overnight

225 g/8 oz parsnips,
peeled and roughly
chopped

225 g/8 oz carrots,
peeled and roughly
chopped

½ lemon

1 tbsp treacle

300 ml/10 fl oz Irish
stout

freshly ground black
pepper

mashed potatoes
and apple sauce
(page 136), to serve

Bacon Cooked with Stout & Root Vegetables

The bacon cooks to a deliciously melting tenderness in the stout and is perfectly complemented by the sweetness of the vegetables and apple sauce.

METHOD

Drain the bacon and scrape the skin. Place the vegetables in a layer on the base of a large, heavy-based saucepan.

Lay the bacon on top of the vegetables, add the lemon, treacle, and pepper, to taste, then add cold water to just cover.

Bring to the boil over a medium heat, then reduce the heat to very low and cook for a further 1 hour.

Add the stout, bring back to the boil and cook for a further 30 minutes.

Serve hot, with mashed potatoes and apple sauce.

SERVES 6–8

INGREDIENTS

2–3 kg/4 lb 8 oz–
6 lb 8 oz ham
leg joint, bone in,
soaked overnight
2 onions, quartered
a handful of cloves
a few green
peppercorns
1 bay leaf
2 tbsp English
mustard powder
85 g/3 oz soft light
brown sugar
1 tsp powdered
mace

Baked Mustard-crusted Ham

Good served hot for a large lunch or dinner party, or cold as part of a buffet.

METHOD

Drain the ham, then place in a large, heavy-based saucepan with the onions, a few of the cloves, the peppercorns and the bay leaf.

Add water to cover, then bring to the boil, skimming off any foam that rises to the surface. Reduce the heat and simmer for 20 minutes per 450 g/1 lb.

Preheat the oven to 190°C/375°F/Gas Mark 5. Remove the ham from the pan and leave to rest for 15–20 minutes.

Use a sharp knife to peel away the skin, then score the fat in a diamond pattern.

Mix the mustard powder, sugar and mace together, then spread evenly over the fat. Stud each diamond with a clove.

Bake in the preheated oven for 30–40 minutes, until the sugar mixture has caramelized.

Remove from the oven and leave to rest for 20 minutes before carving and serving.

SERVES 10–12

INGREDIENTS

1 half leg of lamb, fillet end, about 2 kg/4 lb 8 oz
2 garlic cloves, peeled and sliced
leaves of 1 large fresh rosemary sprig
salt and freshly ground black pepper
roast potatoes (page 116) and cooked spring vegetables, to serve

Gravy
2 tbsp plain flour
125 ml/4 fl oz lamb or beef stock
125 ml/4 fl oz red wine

Roast Lamb

Delicately flavoured with rosemary and garlic, this is the traditional Easter Sunday lunch joint.

METHOD

Preheat the oven to 230°C/450°F/Gas Mark 8. Put the lamb on a rack in a deep roasting tin. Using a sharp knife, make slits in the skin of the joint, about 1 cm/½ inch deep.

Rub salt and pepper all over the skin, then insert the garlic slices and rosemary into the slits.

Roast in the preheated oven for 30 minutes, then reduce the heat to 180°C/350°F/Gas Mark 4 and roast for a further 30 minutes per 450 g/1 lb. Remove from the oven and leave to rest for 20 minutes.

Meanwhile, to make the gravy, pour off most of the fat from the tin, then sprinkle the flour over the remaining sediment. Whisk over a medium heat until smooth, then gradually whisk in the stock and wine. Bring to the boil and bubble until reduced and thickened.

Carve the lamb into slices and serve on warmed plates with gravy, roast potatoes and vegetables.

SERVES 6

INGREDIENTS

1 free-range chicken,
about 1.8 kg/4 lb
85 g/3 oz butter
4 streaky bacon
rashers
salt and freshly
ground black pepper
roast potatoes (page
116), buttered baby
carrots (page 122)
and French beans,
to serve

Gravy

2 tbsp plain flour
250 ml/9 fl oz
chicken stock

Roast Chicken with Gravy

These days, when chicken is so cheap,
it's hard to believe that roast chicken was
once a rare Sunday lunch treat. Buy a free-
range bird and you'll understand why.

METHOD

Preheat the oven to 190°C/375°F/Gas Mark 5. Spread the butter
all over the top of the chicken and season with salt and pepper.
Lay the bacon rashers on the breast, overlapping slightly.

Place the chicken in a roasting tin and roast in the preheated
oven for 20 minutes per 450 g/1 lb, basting with the cooking
juices every 30 minutes. Remove the bacon after 1 hour.
Increase the oven temperature to 220°C/425°F/Gas Mark 7 20
minutes before the end of the cooking time. Remove from the
oven and leave to rest for 10 minutes before serving.

Meanwhile, make the gravy. Pour off most of the fat from the tin,
then sprinkle the flour over the sediment in the tin. Whisk over
a medium heat until smooth, then gradually whisk in the stock.
Bring to the boil and bubble until reduced and thickened.

Carve the chicken and serve with roast potoatoes, carrots and
French beans, with the gravy to hand separately.

*GRANNY'S TIP: To check that the chicken is fully cooked, insert a skewer
into the thickest part of the thigh – if the juices run clear, it is cooked.*

SERVES 6

INGREDIENTS

1 whole side of wild salmon, about 1.3 kg/3 lb, scaled and pin-boned

2 tsp coarse salt

1 tsp freshly ground white pepper

1 lemon, very thinly sliced

4 tbsp olive oil

boiled new potatoes and Hollandaise sauce, to serve

Baked Salmon

In early summer, you might have been lucky enough to come across some line-caught salmon. Nothing compared to that sublime once-a-year eating experience!

METHOD

Preheat the oven to 220°C/425°F/Gas Mark 7. Place the salmon skin side down on a piece of foil large enough to fold over and close at both ends.

Sprinkle over the salt and pepper and lay the lemon slices along the centre of the fish. Drizzle over the oil, then fold over the foil and crimp the edges together to seal tightly.

Bake in the preheated oven for 15 minutes, or until cooked through but still moist.

Serve immediately, with potatoes and Hollandaise sauce.

SERVES 6–8

GRANNY'S TIP: This is also delicious served cold as part of a buffet.

INGREDIENTS

4 very fresh mackerel, filleted, skin on
2 tbsp butter
salt and freshly ground black pepper
fried potatoes (see page 118), to serve

Gooseberry Sauce
25 g/1 oz butter
250 g/9 oz gooseberries, topped and tailed
1 tsp sugar
salt and freshly ground black pepper

Pan-fried Mackerel with Gooseberry Sauce

No childhood holiday on the Irish coast was complete without the mouthwatering aroma of freshly caught mackerel being fried in butter.

METHOD

To make the gooseberry sauce, heat the butter in a small saucepan, add the gooseberries, cover and cook over a medium heat for 20 minutes, or until tender.

Mash the gooseberries, add the sugar and season with salt and pepper. Cook for a further few minutes, then remove from the heat and keep warm until ready to serve.

Melt the butter in a frying pan over a medium heat. Season the fish with salt and pepper, add to the pan and fry for 4–5 minutes on each side, or until the flesh is cooked through and the skin is crispy.

Serve immediately with fried potatoes and gooseberry sauce.

SERVES 4

INGREDIENTS

100 g/3½ oz butter, softened
1 tbsp chopped fresh flat-leaf parsley
1 tsp chopped fresh rosemary
4 trout fillets
olive oil, for greasing
salt and freshly ground black pepper
boiled new potatoes and lemon wedges, to serve

Trout with Herb Butter

This is a lovely way to cook trout – the butter keeps the fish moist, and the herbs are subtle enough not to overpower the delicate flavour.

METHOD

Preheat the oven to 200°C/400°F/Gas Mark 6. Line a baking tray with foil and grease the foil.

Put the butter into a bowl with the parsley and rosemary and mix well until combined. Season with salt and plenty of pepper.

Place the trout fillets on the prepared tray, skin side down, and spread with the parsley butter.

Bake in the preheated oven for 8–10 minutes, until the fish is opaque and just flaking.

Transfer the fish to warmed plates and serve immediately with new potatoes and lemon wedges.

SERVES 4

Creamy Fish Pie

Cod would have been the traditional ingredient in this pie, but you could use any other white fish. Prawns are not strictly necessary, but they add lovely colour, flavour and texture.

INGREDIENTS

650 g/1 lb 7 oz white fish fillets, skinned

250 g/9 oz cooked, peeled prawns (optional)

200 g/7 oz spinach, cooked, drained and finely chopped

55 g/2 oz butter, plus extra for greasing

1 onion, finely chopped

150 ml/5 fl oz single cream

1 tbsp English mustard powder

juice of 1 lemon

creamy mashed potatoes, for topping

salt and freshly ground black pepper

METHOD

Preheat the oven to 180°C/350°F/Gas Mark 4. Grease a 2-litre/3½-pint baking dish.

Cut the fish into bite-sized pieces and place in the base of the prepared dish. Scatter over the prawns, if using, and the spinach and season to taste with salt and pepper.

Melt the butter in a saucepan, add the onion and fry over a medium heat until softened. Add the cream and mustard powder and slowly stir in the lemon juice. Bring to the boil, stirring, then remove from the heat.

Pour the mixture into the dish, making sure that the fish and prawns are evenly covered.

Layer the mashed potatoes onto the fish mixture, then bake in the preheated oven for 15–20 minutes, until the topping is golden. Serve immediately.

SERVES 6

INGREDIENTS

225 g/8 oz self-
raising flour, plus
extra for dusting
pinch of salt
200 ml/7 fl oz cold
lager
vegetable oil, for
deep-frying
3 large potatoes,
peeled and sliced
into thick chips
2 thick white fish
fillets
salt and freshly
ground black pepper
tartare sauce and
lemon wedges, to
serve

SERVES 2

Fish & Chips

The secret to this dish is a light beer
batter, made without any water, and chips
that are fried not once, but twice.

METHOD

Sift the flour and salt into a large bowl. Make a well in the
centre and gradually add the lager, drawing in the flour from
the sides of the bowl. Set aside for 1 hour.

Pour enough oil for deep-frying into a deep saucepan and heat
to 180°C/350°F, or until a cube of bread turns golden and crisp
in 30 seconds. Add the chips and fry for 8–10 minutes. Remove
from the pan, drain on kitchen paper and keep warm.

Reheat the oil to 180°C/350°F. Dip the fish fillets into the batter
to coat, then add them to the oil, one at a time, and fry for 8–10
minutes, turning once, until golden and crisp on the outside.
Remove from the oil using a slotted spoon, drain on kitchen
paper and keep warm.

Reheat the oil to 180°C/350°F. Return the chips to the oil and
fry for 2–3 minutes until golden, then remove and drain on
kitchen paper.

Serve the fish and chips on warmed plates, with tartare sauce
and lemon wedges.

*GRANNY'S TIP: Make sure the temperature of the oil stays at a constant
180°C/350°F – otherwise the fish and chips will be soggy.*

INGREDIENTS

1 cod's roe, about
400 g/14 oz
1 tsp vinegar
2 tbsp plain white
flour
1 egg, beaten
fine dried white
breadcrumbs, for
coating
butter, for frying
salt and freshly
ground black pepper
fried potatoes (page
118) and lemon
wedges, to serve

Pan-fried Cod's Roe

A delicious springtime dish, almost forgotten but now enjoying a long-overdue revival.

METHOD

Put the roe into a saucepan of cold water with the vinegar and a little salt, bring to the boil and cook for 20 minutes. Remove from the heat, drain and leave to cool overnight.

Put the flour into a shallow dish and season with salt and pepper. Put the beaten egg and breadcrumbs into two separate dishes.

Cut the roe into 2-cm/¾-inch thick slices, dip in the flour to coat, then into the egg and, finally, into the breadcrumbs.

Melt some butter in a large frying pan, then add the roe slices and fry for about 5 minutes on each side until golden.

Transfer to warmed plates and serve with fried potatoes and lemon wedges.

SERVES 4

INGREDIENTS

55 g/2 oz seasoned flour
4 cod fillets
2 tbsp vegetable oil
85 g/3 oz butter
juice of 1 lemon
salt and freshly ground black pepper
mashed potatoes and lemon wedges, to serve

Parsley Sauce
300 ml/10 fl oz milk
½ onion, sliced
pinch of freshly grated nutmeg
1 bay leaf
4 whole green peppercorns
35 g/1½ oz butter
25 g/1 oz plain flour
3 tbsp chopped fresh flat-leaf parsley
salt and freshly ground black pepper

SERVES 4

Cod with Parsley Sauce

A simple yet delicious dish – traditionally served on Fridays, when eating meat was prohibited by the Catholic Church.

METHOD

To make the parsley sauce, put the milk, onion, nutmeg, bay leaf and peppercorns into a saucepan and heat until simmering. Remove from the heat and set aside to cool for 8–10 minutes.

Melt 25 g/1 oz of the butter in a heavy-based saucepan. Whisk in the flour until smooth, then cook, whisking constantly, for 1 minute, or until the paste has thickened. Remove from the heat.

Strain the milk mixture into the flour mixture, whisking to incorporate. Return to the heat and gradually bring to the boil, whisking, until thick enough to coat the back of the spoon.

Stir in the remaining butter, then simmer for 2–3 minutes. Stir in the parsley and season with salt and pepper.

Meanwhile, spread the seasoned flour on a plate, add the fish and turn until completely coated.

Heat the oil in a frying pan over a medium heat. Add the fish and fry for 2–3 minutes on each side, or until the flesh is opaque. Dot with butter, sprinkle with lemon juice and remove from the heat.

Transfer the fish to warmed plates, pour over the pan juices and serve with mashed potatoes, lemon wedges and parsley sauce.

INGREDIENTS

butter, for greasing
250 g/9 oz ready-made shortcrust pastry
plain flour, for dusting
6 streaky bacon rashers, chopped
4 large eggs
½ tsp salt
¼ tsp freshly ground black pepper
100 g/3½ oz mature Cheddar cheese, coarsely grated
1 onion, roughly chopped

SERVES 4–6

Bacon & Egg Flan

Nowadays, people call this Quiche Lorraine, but in days gone by it was always known simply as bacon and egg flan.

METHOD

Preheat the oven to 220°C/425°F/Gas Mark 7. Grease a 23-cm/9-inch flan tin.

Dust a work surface with flour and roll out the pastry to around 5 cm/2 inches larger than the tin. Use to line the prepared tin, then trim the pastry to 2.5 cm/1 inch above the rim of the tin. Line with baking paper and bake in the preheated oven for 10 minutes. Remove the paper and bake the pastry case for a further 2 minutes.

Meanwhile, add the bacon to a hot frying pan and fry until cooked to your liking. Beat the eggs with the salt and pepper.

Remove the pastry case from the oven and reduce the oven temperature to 150°C/325°F/Gas Mark 3. Sprinkle the bacon, most of the cheese and the onion over the base of the pastry case. Pour in the egg mixture and sprinkle with the remaining cheese.

Return to the oven and bake for 45–50 minutes, or until a skewer inserted into the centre comes out clean.

Serve warm or cold.

Bacon & Cabbage

The secret to success with this iconic Irish dish is not to overcook the cabbage.

INGREDIENTS

1 kg/2 lb 4 oz back bacon in 1 piece

1 head of white cabbage, cut into quarters

freshly ground black pepper

knob of butter

boiled potatoes and parsley sauce (see page 100), to serve

METHOD

Put the bacon into a large saucepan and add cold water to cover. Bring to the boil, drain, then add more cold water to cover, bring to the boil and simmer for 1 hour.

Add the cabbage and simmer for a further 20 minutes.

Remove the bacon from the pan and slice thinly. Drain the cabbage, season with pepper, then chop roughly and add the butter. Serve with the bacon, boiled potatoes and parsley sauce.

SERVES 4

INGREDIENTS

1 large cauliflower, cut into florets
55 g/2 oz butter, plus extra for greasing
4 tbsp plain flour
500 m/16 fl oz milk
100 g/3½ oz mature Cheddar cheese, coarsely grated
3 tbsp dried breadcrumbs
salt
green salad, to serve

Cauliflower Cheese

This is often served as a side dish, but it is very filling and makes a delicious light main course or lunch dish.

METHOD

Preheat the oven to 200°C/400°F/Gas Mark 6. Grease a deep baking dish.

Bring a saucepan of lightly salted water to the boil, add the cauliflower, bring back to the boil and cook for 5 minutes until just tender. Drain and tip into the prepared baking dish.

Return the pan to the heat, add the butter and heat until melted, then add the flour and stir until a paste forms. Gradually whisk in the milk and bring to the boil, whisking constantly to prevent lumps forming.

Reduce the heat and continue to cook for a further 2–4 minutes, whisking constantly, until thickened. Remove from the heat and stir in most of the cheese.

Pour the sauce over the cauliflower, then scatter over the remaining cheese and the breadcrumbs. Bake in the preheated oven for 20 minutes until golden and bubbling.

Serve hot, accompanied by a green salad.

SERVES 4

SIDE DISHES & ACCOMPANIMENTS

Take a leaf out of Granny's book and always cook vegetables in season to make the most of their natural goodness.

Is minic a mhaolaigh béile maith brón.
A good meal often lessens sadness.

Irish Saying

INGREDIENTS

200 ml/7 fl oz milk
6 spring onions, trimmed and finely chopped
450 g/1 lb shredded green cabbage
450 g/1 lb potatoes, peeled, cooked, drained and mashed
55 g/2 oz butter
salt and freshly ground black pepper

Colcannon

This has similarities with the British bubble and squeak, but this dish is cooked from scratch, not with leftovers.

METHOD

Put the milk into a saucepan, add the onions and cook over a low heat for 5 minutes.

Bring a saucepan of lightly salted water to the boil, add the cabbage, bring back to the boil and cook for 5 minutes, until just tender. Drain and add to the potatoes, mixing to combine.

Add the onion and milk mixture and half the butter. Beat the mixture, season well and serve with the remaining butter dotted on top.

SERVES 4

INGREDIENTS

900 g/2 lb potatoes,
boiled in their
jackets, peeled and
mashed
1 egg, beaten
55 g/2 oz butter
2 tbsp plain flour
pinch of fresh mixed
herbs
milk, if needed
bacon fat, for frying
2 tbsp seasoned
flour
salt and freshly
ground black pepper

Fadge

This hearty bread made with potatoes is delicious served with crisp bacon or to accompany a breakfast fry-up.

METHOD

Put the potatoes into a bowl, add the egg, butter, flour and herbs. Add a little milk if the mixture is too thick. Season to taste with salt and pepper.

Shape the dough into a 2.5-cm/1-inch thick rectangle or round and cut into 8 squares or wedges. Heat the bacon fat in a large, heavy-based frying pan.

Dip each square or wedge in the seasoned flour, add to the pan and fry for 4–5 minutes on each side until golden brown.

Drain on kitchen paper and serve hot.

SERVES 6–8

INGREDIENTS

250 g/9 oz raw potatoes, peeled

250 g/9 oz mashed potatoes

250 g/9 oz plain flour

good pinch of bicarbonate of soda

pinch of salt

225 ml/8 fl oz buttermilk, plus extra if needed

butter, for frying

Boxty

This substantial savoury pancake is made with raw and cooked potatoes and is cooked in butter.

METHOD

Grate the raw potatoes into a colander lined with kitchen paper. Press another sheet of paper on top and squeeze out as much liquid as possible. Mix with the mashed potatoes.

Add the flour, bicarbonate of soda and salt. Mix in enough buttermilk to make a soft batter.

Heat a large, heavy-based frying pan or griddle pan over a high heat, add the butter and heat until melted, then drop in large spoonfuls of the batter. Cook over a medium heat for 3 minutes on each side until golden.

Serve hot.

GRANNY'S TIP: Boxty is usually served plain, but the pancakes can be filled with a stuffing of your choice and served rolled up.

SERVES 4

125 ml/4 fl oz vegetable oil, olive oil, duck fat or goose fat

1.5 kg/3 lb 5 oz potatoes, peeled and quartered

1 tbsp plain flour

salt

Roast Potatoes

A great accompaniment to any roast meat, these will be even more delicious if you use goose or duck fat instead of oil.

METHOD

Preheat the oven to 200°C/400°F/Gas Mark 6. Put the oil into a large roasting tin and place in the oven to heat.

Bring a large saucepan of lightly salted water to the boil, add the potatoes, bring back to the boil and cook for 5 minutes. Remove from the heat and drain in a colander, shaking the potatoes back and forth to fluff up the edges.

Sprinkle the potatoes with the flour and shake until thinly coated.

Carefully add the potatoes to the roasting tin and roll them to coat in the oil. Spread them in the tin in a single layer and roast for 15 minutes. Turn and roast for a further 15 minutes, then turn again and roast for a further 15 minutes, or until golden and crisp on the outside.

Transfer to a warmed dish, season with a little salt and serve immediately.

SERVES 6

GRANNY'S TIP: Be very careful when adding the potatoes to the roasting tin, as the hot fat will spit when it comes in contact with the potatoes.

Fried Potatoes

A good way of using up leftover boiled potatoes, fried potatoes go very well with fried fish and bacon and can even be included in a breakfast fry-up if you're feeling very hungry.

INGREDIENTS

1 small red onion, very finely sliced

500 g/1 lb 2 oz boiled potatoes, cut into 1-cm/½-inch slices

butter, for frying

salt and freshly ground black pepper

fresh rosemary sprig, to garnish

METHOD

Heat the butter in a large, heavy-based frying pan. Add the onion and fry until softened.

Add the potatoes in a single layer, season to taste with salt and pepper and fry, without turning, over a medium heat until golden, then turn and cook on the other side.

Transfer to a warmed dish, garnish with rosemary and serve immediately.

GRANNY'S TIP: If the potatoes have been boiled in their jackets, don't peel them – the fried skin will be crispy and the potatoes will be even more delicious.

SERVES 4

INGREDIENTS

1 large swede,
peeled and cut into
cubes
55 g/2 oz butter
salt and freshly
ground black pepper

Swede Mash

Unfortunate associations with cattle feed put generations of Irish off swede – however, cooked properly, there is little to beat them.

METHOD

Bring a saucepan of lightly salted water to the boil, add the swede, bring back to the boil and cook for 10 minutes until tender.

Remove from the heat and drain.

Add the butter, season to taste with salt and lots of pepper and mash well.

Transfer to a warmed dish and serve immediately.

SERVES 4

INGREDIENTS

500 g/1 lb 10 oz
baby carrots, washed
but not peeled
2 tsp sugar
55 g/2 oz butter
salt and freshly
ground black pepper
chopped fresh
parsley, to garnish

Buttered Baby Carrots

These new season carrots, with their sweet and glossy coating, are a perfect partner for roast lamb or chicken.

METHOD

Put the whole carrots into a saucepan with just enough water to cover, then add the sugar and butter.

Bring to the boil, then reduce the heat and simmer until the water has evaporated and the carrots are tender.

Transfer to a warmed serving dish, season to taste with salt and pepper, garnish with parsley and serve immediately.

SERVES 4–6

GRANNY'S TIP: Take care that the water doesn't boil off before the carrots are cooked – they will burn very easily.

INGREDIENTS

250 g/9 oz carrots,
roughly chopped
450 g/1 lb parsnips,
roughly chopped
55 g/2 oz butter
salt and freshly
ground black pepper
chopped fresh
parsley, to garnish

Carrot & Parsnip Mash

This is traditionally served to accompany the Christmas turkey as an alternative to the ubiquitous Brussels sprouts.

METHOD

Bring a large saucepan of lightly salted water to the boil, add the carrots and parsnips, bring back to the boil and cook until soft and tender.

Drain, then add the butter, season to taste with salt and lots of pepper and mash well.

Transfer to a warmed serving dish, garnish with parsley and serve immediately.

SERVES 6

GRANNY'S TIP: If you like a really smooth mash, purée the mixture in a food processor.

INGREDIENTS

450 g/1 lb shelled
garden peas
1 tsp sugar
1 fresh mint sprig
25 g/1 oz butter
salt
fresh chopped mint,
to garnish

Fresh Peas with Mint

**Nothing says 'summer' quite like peas
fresh from the garden. Cooking and
serving them with a little mint really
brings out their flavour.**

METHOD

Bring a saucepan of lightly salted water to the boil, add the
peas, sugar and mint sprig, bring back to the boil and cook for
about 4 minutes until just tender.

Drain, toss with the butter until melted and transfer to a
warmed serving dish.

Garnish with the chopped mint and serve immediately.

SERVES 6–8

INGREDIENTS

1 red cabbage

1 cooking apple, peeled, cored and roughly chopped

1 red onion, finely chopped

1 tbsp soft light brown sugar

large pinch of mixed spice

½ tsp ground cloves

½ tsp freshly ground nutmeg

150 ml/5 fl oz red wine vinegar

knob of butter

young nettle tips, to garnish

SERVES 6–8

Spiced Red Cabbage

The long slow cooking required for this dish fills the house with the wonderful aroma of spices. This cabbage is perfect with any pork, ham or bacon dish.

METHOD

Preheat the oven to 150°C/300°F/Gas Mark 2.

Remove the tough outer leaves of the cabbage, then cut it into quarters and use a sharp knife to cut out the core. Slice the quarters thinly vertically and place in a large casserole dish.

Add the apple, onion, sugar and spices and pour over the vinegar. Mix everything together well.

Cover tightly and cook in the preheated oven for 2–3 hours, uncovering and stirring occasionally. Add the butter and stir to combine 30 minutes before the end of cooking.

Remove from the oven, transfer to a warmed serving dish and leave to cool a little, then garnish with nettle tips and serve.

GRANNY'S TIP: You can make a double quantity and freeze the surplus for up to a month. Thaw before reheating and toss the warmed cabbage with a small knob of butter to restore its glossiness.

INGREDIENTS

1 Savoy cabbage
85 g/3 oz butter
salt and freshly
ground black pepper

Cabbage Tossed with Butter

Many people have a childhood memory of pungent, overcooked and tasteless cabbage – this way of cooking it is a million miles away from that experience.

METHOD

Remove the tough outer leaves of the cabbage and cut it into quarters. Use a sharp knife to cut out the core, then slice the quarters thinly vertically.

Put a little water, 55 g/2 oz of the butter and some salt into a large saucepan and bring to the boil. Add the cabbage and cook, tossing, over a high heat for 1–2 minutes.

Cover the pan and continue to cook for 1–2 minutes. Remove from the heat, add some pepper and the remaining butter and toss to coat.

Transfer to a warmed serving dish and serve immediately.

SERVES 4

INGREDIENTS

8 small onions,
peeled
350 ml/12 fl oz
double cream
fresh thyme sprigs
salt and freshly
ground black pepper

Onions Baked with Cream

This rich dish raises the humble onion to the realms of gourmet food. It's delicious with roast beef, pork or chicken.

METHOD

Preheat the oven to 180°C/325°F/Gas Mark 4. Bring a large saucepan of lightly salted water to the boil. Add the whole onions, bring back to the boil and bubble for about 20 minutes until tender.

Remove from the heat and drain. Cut the onions in half vertically and place them in a single layer in a baking dish. Scatter over the thyme sprigs, pour in the cream and season to taste with salt and pepper.

Bake in the preheated oven for 20–25 minutes, until bubbling.

Remove the thyme sprigs and serve the onions straight from the baking dish.

SERVES 4

INGREDIENTS

1 small onion,
peeled
3 cloves
300 ml/10 fl oz milk
115 g/4 oz fine
dried white
breadcrumbs
1 tbsp butter
salt and freshly
ground black pepper

Bread Sauce

The perfect accompaniment to turkey or
goose, this dull-sounding sauce has layers
of subtle and interesting flavour.

METHOD

Stud the onion with the cloves. Put the milk in a saucepan, add
the onion, then heat over a low heat until just boiling.

Stir in the breadcrumbs and simmer over a low heat for 15–20
minutes.

Remove the onion, season to taste with salt and pepper, then
stir in the butter, transfer to a warmed sauce boat and serve hot.

SERVES 6–8

INGREDIENTS

2 large Bramley apples, peeled and cored

2 tsp sugar

pinch of ground cinnamon

Apple Sauce

The traditional accompaniment to roast pork, tangy apple sauce goes well with almost all meat dishes.

METHOD

Cut the apples into quarters and slice the quarters.

Place the apple slices in a small saucepan with the sugar, cinnamon and 1–2 tablespoons of water and heat over a low heat until softened. Add a little more water if the apples begin to stick to the base of the pan.

As the apples begin to soften, break them down with a wooden spoon and stir until completely soft. If you like a very smooth sauce, place the cooked apple in a blender or food processor and pulse until smooth.

Transfer to a serving dish and serve warm or cold.

GRANNY'S TIP: Take care not to add too much water – it may seem as if the apples will never break down, but they will, quite suddenly, to make a lovely fluffy apple sauce.

SERVES 4

DESSERTS

Desserts every day are bad for the waistline and bad for the teeth, but Granny knows that we all need the occasional sweet treat.

An rud is annamh is iontach.
What is seldom is wonderful.

Irish Saying

INGREDIENTS

15 g/½ oz
powdered gelatine
(2 sachets)

300 ml/10 fl oz cold
strong coffee

300 ml/10 fl oz Irish
stout

140 g/5 oz lime jelly

dash of irish cream
liqueur

300 ml/10 fl oz
double cream, lightly
whipped

85 g/3 oz soft light
brown sugar

300 g/10½ oz
canned mandarin
oranges, drained, to
decorate

SERVES 4

St Patrick's Day Jelly

This colourful jelly satisfies several of
the requirements for a St Patrick's Day
celebration – it's green, white and orange
and infused with alcohol!

METHOD

Soak the gelatine in 5 tablespoons of cold water for 5 minutes.
Place in a saucepan with the coffee and stout and heat over a
low heat, stirring constantly. Do not allow to boil. Divide the
warm liquid among 4 glass dishes. Leave to cool, then chill
overnight.

Prepare the lime jelly according to the packet instructions and
pour it into a flat, rectangular dish. Chill overnight.

Chop the lime jelly into small pieces and scatter them over the
coffee and stout jelly.

Add the liqueur to the cream and add to the bowls. Sprinkle
with sugar, decorate with mandarin orange segments and serve.

INGREDIENTS

85 g/3 oz fresh
wholemeal
breadcrumbs
butter, for greasing
85 g/3 oz granulated
sugar
4 tbsp water
450 ml/16 fl oz
double cream
55 g/2 oz icing
sugar, sifted
2 tbsp dark rum
1 tsp vanilla extract

Brown Bread Ice Cream

This deliciously crunchy ice cream is very simple to make and, unlike many ice creams, doesn't require frequent removal from the freezer for stirring.

METHOD

Spread the breadcrumbs on a baking tray and toast under a hot grill until golden brown. Leave to cool. Grease a separate baking tray.

Put the sugar and water into a saucepan and heat over a low heat until the sugar has dissolved. Bring to the boil and bubble until the syrup is a rich caramel colour. Remove from the heat and stir in the breadcrumbs.

Turn out onto the prepared tray and leave to harden. Break the caramel into pieces and grind using a pestle and mortar.

Whip the cream until soft peaks hold, then beat in the icing sugar, rum and vanilla extract. Fold in the crumbs, pour into a freezerproof container, cover and freeze for at least 3–4 hours without stirring.

SERVES 6

INGREDIENTS

85 g/3 oz butter, melted

225 g/8 oz digestive biscuit crumbs

700 g/1 lb 9 oz cream cheese, softened

115 g/4 oz sugar

3 eggs, beaten

2 tbsp plain flour

225 ml/8 fl oz Irish cream liqueur

1 tsp vanilla extract

SERVES 8–10

Irish Cream Cheesecake

This plain cheesecake is given a luxurious touch with the addition of a healthy glug of Irish cream liqueur.

METHOD

Preheat the oven to 180°C/350°F/Gas Mark 4. Mix the butter and biscuit crumbs together and press into the base of a 20-cm/8-inch round springform cake tin. Bake in the preheated oven for 5 minutes. Remove from the oven (do not switch off the oven).

Meanwhile, put the cheese and sugar into a bowl and mix to combine, then add the eggs, flour, liqueur and vanilla extract and beat until smooth.

Pour the mixture onto the crumb base, return to the oven and bake for 40 minutes. Leave to cool, then chill overnight.

INGREDIENTS

225 g/8 oz ready-made shortcrust pastry

3 eggs

450 g/1 lb curd cheese or cottage cheese

4 tbsp caster sugar

30 g/1 oz butter, softened, plus extra for greasing

finely grated zest and juice of 1 small lemon

1 tsp vanilla extract

1 tbsp plain flour, plus extra for dusting

Curd Cake

This is an old Irish version of baked cheesecake – the curd cheese gives it a unique texture. Nowadays, cottage cheese is more readily available and is a good substitute for the curd cheese.

METHOD

Preheat the oven to 180°C/350°F/Gas Mark 4 and grease a 20-cm/8-inch round loose-based tart tin. Roll out the pastry on a lightly floured work surface, then use to line the prepared tin.

Separate 2 of the eggs and beat the yolks, then whisk the whites until stiff peaks hold. Put the cheese, 3 tablespoons of the sugar, half the butter and the egg yolks into a bowl and mix to combine.

Stir in the lemon zest and juice and the vanilla extract. Beat well, then gradually fold in the egg whites.

Spread the filling evenly in the pastry case. Melt the remaining butter and mix with the remaining egg and sugar and the flour. Spread evenly over the filling.

Bake in the preheated oven for 35–40 minutes, or until golden brown. Leave to cool in the tin, then turn out, cut into wedges and serve.

SERVES 8

GRANNY'S TIP: Leave the cake on the base of the tin to serve.

INGREDIENTS

225 g/8 oz butter
1 kg/2 lb 4 oz
Bramley apples,
peeled, cored and
thinly sliced
115 g/4 oz sugar
1 tbsp lemon juice
grated rind of 1
lemon
2 egg yolks, beaten
10 slices of day-old
white bread, crusts
removed
whipped cream, to
serve

Apple Charlotte

A delicious autumn dessert that makes good use of day-old bread.

METHOD

Preheat the oven to 200°C/400°F/Gas Mark 6. Melt half the butter in a large, heavy-based saucepan over a medium heat. Add the apples, sugar, lemon juice, lemon rind and about 3 tablespoons of water. Bring to the boil over a medium heat, then reduce the heat, cover and cook for about 20–25 minutes until the apples are soft. Uncover, increase the heat to high and cook vigorously for 5 minutes.

Remove from the heat and stir in the egg yolks. Melt the remaining butter and use some of it to brush the sides and base of a 23-cm/9-inch round springform cake tin. Line the base with baking paper.

Cut the bread into strips 3 cm/1¼ inches wide and as tall as the tin. Dip in the remaining melted butter and arrange over the base and around the sides of the tin, reserving some for the top. Spoon in the apple, then place the remaining bread on top.

Bake in the preheated oven for 20 minutes, then reduce the oven temperature to 190°C/375°F/Gas Mark 5 and bake for a further 35 minutes until the top is a deep golden brown.

Leave to cool for 15 minutes, then unclip and remove the springform. Serve warm or cold with whipped cream.

SERVES 6

INGREDIENTS

450 g/1 lb Bramley apples, peeled and cored

3 tbsp caster sugar

2 egg whites

250 ml/9 fl oz whipped cream

chopped toasted hazelnuts, to decorate

Apple Snow

This is very simple to make and is a great way of using egg whites that have been left over from other recipes.

METHOD

Put the apples and sugar into a saucepan with 1–2 teaspoons of water and cook over a medium heat until the apples are soft.

Whisk the egg whites until soft peaks hold.

Fold the egg white and cream into the apples, then spoon into 4 individual glasses and chill for 20–30 minutes before serving.

Sprinkle with toasted hazelnuts and serve.

SERVES 4

INGREDIENTS

450 g/1 lb
gooseberries, topped
and tailed
225 g/8 oz sugar
500 ml/16 fl oz
whipped cream
chopped hazelnuts,
to decorate

Gooseberry Fool

This light dessert is simplicity itself and has a real taste of summer.

METHOD

Cook the gooseberries with the sugar and a little water for about 5 minutes until the fruit is just bursting.

Purée the gooseberries, then set aside and leave to cool.

Gradually fold the cream into the fruit, then spoon into glasses and chill for 20–30 minutes.

Sprinkle with chopped nuts and serve.

SERVES 6

GRANNY'S TIP: Replace the cooked gooseberries with an equal quantity of stewed rhubarb to make a delicious Rhubarb Fool.

INGREDIENTS

butter, for greasing
plain flour, for
dusting
250 g/9 oz ready-
made shortcrust
pastry
450 g/9 oz home-
made strawberry
jam (page 226) or
raspberry jam
milk, for brushing
whipped cream or
custard, to serve

Jam Tart

This is a great standby dessert for unexpected guests. It's most attractive when made with a red jam, although any jam can be used.

METHOD

Preheat the oven to 200°C/400°F/Gas Mark 6 and grease a 20-cm/8-inch tart tin.

Roll out the pastry on a floured work surface and use to line the prepared tin. Chill until needed. Re-roll the pastry trimmings and cut out 8 strips that are slightly longer than the diameter of the tin.

Heat the jam over a low heat until warm, then spread over the pastry case. Weave the pastry strips into a lattice pattern over the top, pressing the ends into the edge of the pastry case. Brush with a little milk.

Bake in the preheated oven for about 30 minutes until the pastry is golden.

Leave to cool for 30 minutes, then cut into wedges and serve with whipped cream.

SERVES 6–8

GRANNY'S TIP: Always allow jam to cool before serving – jam retains heat very efficiently and can give you a nasty burn.

INGREDIENTS

butter, for greasing
450 g/1 lb ready-made shortcrust pastry
beaten egg, for brushing
1 kg/2 lb 4 oz Bramley apples, peeled, cored and diced
450 g/1 lb blackberries
125 g/4 oz caster sugar
1 tbsp plain flour, plus extra for dusting
pinch of ground nutmeg
pinch of ground cinnamon
icing sugar, for sprinkling
whipped cream or vanilla ice cream, to serve

SERVES 6–8

Blackberry & Apple Tart

A lovely tart that makes the most of the fruits of late summer and autumn.

METHOD

Preheat the oven to 190°C/375°F/Gas Mark 5. Grease a 36 x 12-cm/14 x 4½-inch rectangular tart tin.

Roll out the pastry on a floured work surface and use it to line the prepared tin. Prick with a fork. Line with baking paper and baking beans and bake in the preheated oven for 20 minutes. Remove the paper and beans, brush the pastry case with some of the beaten egg and return to the oven to bake for a further 10 minutes. Remove from the oven (do not switch off the oven).

Meanwhile, put the apples into a saucepan with the blackberries and sugar and heat until softened. Remove from the heat, stir in the flour, nutmeg and cinnamon, then pile into the pastry case, spreading evenly.

Re-roll the pastry trimmings and cut out 8 strips that are slightly longer than the length of the tin. Weave the pastry strips into a lattice pattern over the top, pushing the ends into the tart. Brush the strips with beaten egg.

Return to the oven and bake for 55–60 minutes until the pastry is golden and the filling is bubbling. Leave to cool for at least 30 minutes, then sprinkle with icing sugar and serve with cream.

INGREDIENTS

butter, for greasing
250 g/9 oz ready-made shortcrust pastry
plain flour, for dusting
150 g/5 oz fresh white breadcrumbs
225 ml/8 fl oz golden syrup
beaten egg, for brushing
golden caster sugar, for sprinkling
whipped cream or vanilla ice cream, to serve

Golden Syrup Tart

Golden syrup has been a staple store cupboard ingredient in Ireland for more than fifty years, so it was always easy to make this delicious tart at short notice.

METHOD

Preheat the oven to 180°C/350°F/Gas Mark 4. Grease a 20-cm/8-inch round loose-based tart tin.

Roll out the pastry on a floured work surface and use to line the prepared tin.

Mix the breadcrumbs and golden syrup together and spread evenly in the pastry case.

Re-roll the pastry trimmings and cut out several 5-mm/¼-inch wide strips, slightly longer than the diameter of the tin. Weave the pastry strips into a lattice pattern over the top of the tart, pressing the ends into the edge of the pastry case.

Bake in the preheated oven for 20 minutes. Brush the pastry with beaten egg, then return to the oven for a further 15 minutes, or until the pastry is golden.

Leave to cool for 15–20 minutes, then sprinkle with icing sugar, slice and serve with cream.

SERVES 6–8

INGREDIENTS

85 g/3 oz raisins or sultanas

25 g/1 oz demerara sugar

½ tsp ground nutmeg or cinnamon

100 g/3½ oz butter, softened

6 eating apples, cored

vanilla ice cream or custard, to serve

Baked Apples

A deliciously healthy dessert, so easy a child could make it!

METHOD

Preheat the oven to 150°C/300°C/Gas Mark 2.

Put the raisins into a bowl with the sugar, add the nutmeg and stir to combine.

Add the butter and mix well. Spoon the mixture into the holes in the apples, pressing in well.

Stand the apples in a baking dish, cover with foil and bake in the preheated oven for 35–40 minutes. Remove the foil and cook for a further 20 minutes until the apples are soft.

Transfer to plates and serve with ice cream.

SERVES 6

Rhubarb Crumble

The rhubarb season is very short, so make sure you take advantage of it by making this delicious crumble.

INGREDIENTS

450 g/1 lb trimmed rhubarb, cut into 2.5-cm/1-inch lengths

100 g/3½ oz caster sugar

150 g/5½ oz self-raising flour

85 g/3 oz butter, at room temperature

55 g/2 oz demerara sugar

55 g/2 oz hazelnuts, finely chopped

vanilla ice cream or custard, to serve

METHOD

Put the rhubarb into a saucepan with the caster sugar and 2–3 tablespoons of water. Cook over a low heat for about 15 minutes until the rhubarb is soft but not disintegrating. Transfer to a baking dish.

Meanwhile, preheat the oven to 200°C/400°F/Gas Mark 6. Sift the flour into a bowl, cut in the butter and mix with your fingertips until soft and crumbly.

Add the sugar and nuts and mix to combine, then sprinkle the mixture over the rhubarb.

Bake in the preheated oven for 30 minutes.

Serve hot, with ice cream.

SERVES 6

Carrageen Pudding

Carrageen moss is a type of seaweed found on the Irish coast. It produces a gel when heated, which makes it a good vegetarian alternative to gelatine.

INGREDIENTS

500 ml/16 fl oz milk
250 ml/9 fl oz double cream
55 g/2 oz dried carrageen moss, washed
1 tsp vanilla extract
100 g/3½ oz caster sugar
mint leaves, to decorate

METHOD

Put the milk and cream into a saucepan over a medium heat. Add the carrageen moss and stir until it releases its jelly.

Add the vanilla extract and sugar and cook, stirring, for a further 5 minutes.

Remove from the heat, strain into glasses or small bowls and chill until set. Decorate each glass with a mint leaf and serve.

SERVES 4

INGREDIENTS

butter, for greasing
55 g/2 oz caster
sugar
2 large eggs, beaten
55 g/2 oz plain flour,
plus extra for dusting
1 tbsp raspberry jam
400 g/14 oz fresh
sliced fruit, such as
strawberries and
peaches, or canned
fruit, such as peach
slices or fruit cocktail
whipped cream, to
serve

Fruit Flan

In the 1960s and 1970s fruit flan was usually made with a ready-made flan case and canned fruit. However, making the case from scratch is easy and the result is ten times better.

METHOD

Preheat the oven to 200°C/400°F/Gas Mark 6. Grease a 20-cm/8-inch round flan tin with butter and dust it with flour, shaking out any excess.

Put the sugar and eggs into a bowl set over a saucepan of gently simmering water and whisk until pale and creamy.

Remove from the heat and sift in the flour, folding it in with a metal spoon.

Pour the batter into the prepared tin and bake in the preheated oven for 10–15 minutes until golden.

Leave to cool in the tin for 10 minutes, then turn out onto a wire rack and leave until cold. Spread the jam on the base of the sponge, then arrange the fruit attractively on top and serve immediately with whipped cream.

SERVES 6–8

INGREDIENTS

450 g/1 lb
raspberries,
loganberries,
blueberries,
strawberries or a
mixture, roughly
chopped

55 g/2 oz caster
sugar

500 ml/16 fl oz
whipped cream

boudoir biscuits, to
serve

Summer Fruit Fluff

Made in moments, this is a delicious way to use the abundance of soft fruit that appears in the summer months.

METHOD

Sprinkle the fruit with the sugar, then fold in the cream.

Divide among six glasses and serve immediately with boudoir biscuits.

SERVES 6

INGREDIENTS

butter, for greasing
8-10 slices day-old
white bread, crusts
removed
600 g/1 lb 5 oz
mixed summer
berries
100 g/3½ oz sugar
pouring cream, to
serve

Summer Pudding

Stale bread and summer berries may seem an unlikely combination, but this pudding tastes heavenly.

METHOD

Grease a 1.2-litre/2-pint pudding basin. Place a piece of bread in the base, then overlap the remaining slices around the sides, reserving 2 slices for the top.

Put the fruit into a saucepan with the sugar and heat gently until the juices are beginning to run.

Pour the fruit and juice into the basin, reserving some of the juice. Cover the top with the remaining bread slices, then place a plate and a weight on top. Chill overnight.

Turn out the chilled pudding onto a plate, then pour the reserved juice over any white patches and serve with cream.

SERVES 6

GRANNY'S TIP: For a touch of luxury, add a little fruit liqueur, such as crème de cassis, to the fruit before pouring it into the basin.

INGREDIENTS

125 g/4½ oz
pudding rice
400 ml/14 fl
oz sweetened
condensed milk
600 ml/1 pint milk
knob of butter, plus
extra for greasing
whole nutmeg, for
grating

Baked Rice Puddings

This everyday dessert used to be made in
a pudding basin and served at the table,
but these individual little puddings are far
more attractive.

METHOD

Preheat the oven to 150°C/300°F/Gas Mark 2. Grease 6 ramekins
with butter.

Divide the rice among the prepared ramekins. Mix the
condensed milk and milk together in a jug and pour the
mixture over the rice.

Dot the butter on top and grate over a little nutmeg.

Bake in the preheated oven for 30 minutes, then stir and bake
for a further 30 minutes–1 hour, until the rice grains have
swollen and a golden skin has formed on top.

Serve the puddings hot.

SERVES 6

Semolina

This very light milk dessert is usually served with jam or fresh fruit for colour and extra flavour.

METHOD

Mix the semolina with a little of the milk to form a paste.

Put the remaining milk into a large saucepan and bring to the boil over a medium heat.

Reduce the heat, add the semolina paste, sugar and vanilla extract and stir until thick.

Spoon into individual glasses, decorate with strawberry slices and mint and serve warm.

SERVES 4

INGREDIENTS

100 g/3½ oz butter, softened, plus extra for greasing

100 g/3½ oz caster sugar

2 eggs, beaten

1 tsp vanilla extract

100 g/3½ oz self-raising flour, sifted

125 g/4 oz home-made marmalade (page 230)

custard, to serve

SERVES 4

Steamed Marmalade Pudding

This is probably the ultimate comfort food, the perfect dessert on a cold winter's night.

METHOD

Grease a 600-ml/1-pint pudding basin. Cream the butter and sugar together until light and fluffy. Gradually beat in the eggs, then add the vanilla extract and mix until combined.

Gently fold in the flour and mix well.

Put the marmalade into the base of the prepared basin, then spoon in the batter. Cover the basin with a round of greaseproof paper, pleated in the middle, and tie on securely with string.

Place the basin in a saucepan of simmering water and steam for 1½ hours, topping up the saucepan with boiling water as necessary.

Remove the basin from the saucepan and cut away the paper and string. Run a knife around the sides of the pudding to release it, then turn it out onto a plate and serve with custard.

GRANNY'S TIP: This pudding works just as well with jam – simply substitute the marmalade with an equal quantity of your favourite flavour.

Bread & Butter Pudding

**A warming and filling winter dessert –
you can add a little touch of luxury by
replacing half the milk with single cream.**

INGREDIENTS

6 thin slices of
white bread, crusts
removed
55 g/2 oz butter,
plus extra for
greasing
55 g/2 oz currants
55 g/2 oz sultanas
55 g/2 oz caster
sugar
2 eggs
600 ml/1 pint milk
custard, to serve

METHOD

Spread the bread with the butter and cut into triangles. Grease
a 1-litre/1¾-pint ovenproof dish and arrange half the bread
triangles in the base. Sprinkle with the currants, sultanas and
half the sugar.

Top with the remaining bread, buttered side up, and sprinkle
with the remaining sugar.

Beat the eggs and milk together and pour over the bread. Leave
to stand for 30 minutes.

Meanwhile, preheat the oven to 160°C/325°F/Gas Mark 3. Bake
the pudding for 45–60 minutes until set and browned on top.

Serve hot, with custard.

SERVES 4

BREADS, CAKES & BISCUITS

With Granny's selection of oven-fresh breads and scones, luscious cakes and delicious biscuits, you can ease those hunger pangs at any time of the day.

Is maith an t-anlann an t-ocras.
Hunger is a great sauce.

Irish Saying

INGREDIENTS
450 g/1 lb plain
white flour, plus
extra for dusting
1 tsp salt
1 tsp bicarbonate
of soda
400 ml/14 fl oz
buttermilk

White Soda Bread

Soda bread is a distinctly Irish bread –
unlike yeast bread it does not respond
well to too much handling, so don't
overwork the dough.

METHOD

Preheat the oven to 230°C/450°F/Gas Mark 8. Dust a baking
sheet with flour.

Mix the dry ingredients in a large mixing bowl, then make a
well in the centre and gradually add the buttermilk, drawing in
the dry ingredients from the sides of the bowl. Mix until a moist
dough forms.

Turn the dough out onto a floured work surface and shape it
into a round about 5 cm/2 inches high. Place the round on the
prepared baking sheet and use a floured knife to cut a deep
cross in it.

Bake in the preheated oven for 30–45 minutes until the loaf
sounds hollow when tapped on the base.

MAKES 1 LOAF

INGREDIENTS

675 g/1 lb 8 oz wholemeal flour

450 g/1 lb strong white flour, plus extra for dusting

2 tsp bicarbonate of soda

2 tsp salt

750 m/1½ pints buttermilk, plus extra if needed

Brown Soda Bread

A wholemeal alternative to white soda bread. Wholemeal flour on its own would make a very dense loaf, so white flour is added to the mixture.

METHOD

Preheat the oven to 230°C/450°F/Gas Mark 8. Dust a large baking sheet with flour.

Mix the dry ingredients in a large mixing bowl, then make a well in the centre and gradually add the buttermilk, drawing in the dry ingredients from the sides of the bowl. Mix until a soft dough forms, adding more buttermilk if necessary. The dough should not be too moist.

Turn the dough out onto a floured work surface, divide into 2 pieces and shape both pieces into a round about 5 cm/2 inches high. Place on the prepared baking sheet and use a floured knife to cut a deep cross in each loaf.

Bake in the preheated oven for 15–20 minutes, then reduce the oven temperature to 200°C/400°F/Gas Mark 6 and bake for a further 20–25 minutes until the loaves sound hollow when tapped on the base.

MAKES 2 LOAVES

INGREDIENTS

vegetable oil, for greasing
1.3 kg/3 lb wholemeal flour
500 ml/18 fl oz water
500 ml/18 fl oz milk
1 tbsp soft light brown sugar
55 g/2 oz fresh yeast
2 tsp salt
milk, for brushing
sunflower seeds, for sprinkling

Brown Bread

A lovely, nutty yeast bread with a slightly sweet flavour. It's well worth taking the time to make it with fresh yeast.

METHOD

Grease two 900-g/2-lb loaf tins and the inside of 2 large polythene bags.

Put half the flour into a large mixing bowl. Mix the milk and water together in a jug, then add the sugar and yeast. Add to the flour and beat well. Cover the bowl with a damp tea towel and leave to stand for 10–15 minutes, until the mixture is frothy.

Add the remaining flour and the salt and mix until a soft dough forms. Knead for 10 minutes.

Divide the dough into 2 pieces and place in the prepared tins. Put the tins into the prepared bags and leave to stand until the dough has risen to the top of the tins. Meanwhile, preheat the oven to 230°C/450°F/Gas Mark 8.

Brush the tops of the loaves with milk, sprinkle with sunflower seeds and bake in the preheated oven for 30–40 minutes until they are risen and golden brown and sound hollow when tapped on the base.

MAKES 2 LOAVES

Griddle Bread

This is a very old Irish bread recipe, traditionally cooked on a cast-iron griddle over the fire.

INGREDIENTS

450 g/1 lb self-raising flour, plus extra for dusting

pinch of salt

250–350 ml/ 9–12 fl oz buttermilk

METHOD

Sift the flour and salt together into a bowl. Make a well in the centre and gradually add the buttermilk until a soft, wet dough forms.

Heat a dry, flat cast-iron griddle pan over a high heat, then reduce the heat to low and dust the pan with flour.

Put the dough into the pan, spreading it out with wet hands until it covers the surface of the pan.

Cook the bread for 10 minutes on each side, or until it is brown in patches. Place on a wire rack to cool slightly and serve warm, cut into wedges.

SERVES 4–6

GRANNY'S TIP: If you don't have any self-raising flour, use plain flour and add 1 teaspoon of bicarbonate of soda.

Buttermilk Scones

These lovely scones are perfect for serving at afternoon tea, with lashings of butter and jam.

INGREDIENTS

450 g/1 lb self-raising flour, plus extra for dusting

pinch of salt

100 g/3½ oz chilled butter, diced

85 g/3 oz caster sugar

300 m/10 fl oz buttermilk

milk, for brushing

METHOD

Preheat the oven to 220°C/425°F/Gas Mark 7. Dust a baking sheet with flour.

Put the flour, salt and butter into a bowl and rub in with your fingertips until the mixture forms fine crumbs. Add the sugar and mix to combine.

Heat the buttermilk over a low heat until lukewarm. Gradually add to the flour mixture, cutting it in with a knife until just combined.

Turn out the dough onto a floured work surface and bring it together with your hands. Press it out to a thickness of 4 cm/1½ inches with your hands, then use a 6-cm/2½-inch round biscuit cutter to cut out 12 rounds, reshaping the trimmings as necessary.

Place the scones on the prepared baking sheet, then brush with a little milk and bake in the preheated oven for 10–12 minutes until golden. Remove from the oven and transfer to a wire rack to cool slightly. Serve warm.

MAKES 12

INGREDIENTS

85 g/3 oz butter, plus extra for greasing

150 g/5½ oz caster sugar

2 eggs, beaten

4 very ripe bananas, mashed well

225 g/8 oz self-raising flour

1 tsp mixed spice

1 tsp salt

Banana Bread

This delicious cut-and-come-again loaf was clearly inspired by a bowl of very ripe, blackening bananas – the blacker the better, for this recipe!

METHOD

Preheat the oven to 180°C/350°F/Gas Mark 4. Grease a 900-g/2-lb loaf tin with butter.

Put the butter into a bowl and cream until soft, then add the eggs and sugar and beat until smooth.

Add the bananas and stir to combine. Sift in the flour, spice and salt and mix well.

Pour into the prepared tin and bake in the preheated oven for 1 hour–1 hour 10 minutes until golden brown. Cover with a piece of foil if the top is browning too quickly.

GRANNY'S TIP: If you like your banana bread to have a bit more texture, stir 55 g/2 oz chopped walnuts into the batter.

MAKES 1 LOAF

INGREDIENTS

225 g/8 oz butter, plus extra for greasing

225 g/8 oz soft light brown sugar

300 ml/10 fl oz Irish stout

225 g/8 oz raisins

225 g/8 oz sultanas

115 g/4 oz chopped mixed peel

450 g/1 lb plain flour

½ tsp bicarbonate of soda

½ tsp ground allspice

½ tsp ground nutmeg

115 g/4 oz glacé cherries, rinsed, dried and halved

finely grated rind of 1 lemon

3 eggs, beaten

SERVES 12

Porter Cake

A rich fruit cake, steeped in stout for extra depth of flavour.

METHOD

Preheat the oven to 180°C/350°F/Gas Mark 4. Grease a 25-cm/10-inch deep round cake tin with butter and line with baking paper.

Put the butter, sugar and stout into a saucepan and heat over a low heat until the butter is melted. Add the raisins, sultanas and mixed peel, bring to the boil, then simmer for 10 minutes.

Leave to cool, then add the flour, bicarbonate of soda, spices, cherries and lemon rind. Gradually add the eggs and mix well to combine.

Pour into the prepared tin and bake in the preheated oven for about 1½ hours until a skewer inserted into the centre comes out clean. Leave to cool in the tin.

GRANNY'S TIP: This cake keeps well – wrap it in foil and store in an airtight tin for up to 2 weeks.

INGREDIENTS

450 g/1lb plain flour
½ tsp freshly grated
nutmeg
pinch of salt
15 g/½ oz fresh
yeast
55 g/2 oz soft light
brown sugar
300 ml/10 fl oz
lukewarm milk
2 eggs, beaten
55 g/2 oz butter,
plus extra for
greasing
115 g/4 oz chopped
mixed peel
225 g/8 oz currants
225 g/8 oz raisins
1 egg yolk, beaten,
for glazing
butter, to serve

SERVES 10–12

Barm Brack

Made with yeast, this traditional Halloween delicacy is a sweet bread rather than a cake. It used to be filled with symbolic favours, but these are now omitted for reasons of health and safety.

METHOD

Grease a 20-cm/8-inch round cake tin with butter. Sift the flour, nutmeg and salt together into a large mixing bowl.

In a separate bowl, blend the yeast with 1 teaspoon of the sugar and a little of the milk until it froths.

Add the remaining sugar to the flour mixture. Add the remaining milk to the yeast mixture, then add to the flour mixture with the eggs and butter. Mix with a wooden spoon for about 10 minutes until stiff.

Fold in the dried fruit, then transfer the batter to the prepared tin. Cover with a damp tea towel and leave to rise for about 1 hour until doubled in size.

Meanwhile, preheat the oven to 200°C/400°F/Gas Mark 6. Bake the brack in the preheated oven for 1 hour, then glaze with the beaten egg yolk and bake for a further 5 minutes.

Transfer to a wire rack and leave to cool, then slice and serve with butter.

Tea Cake

Tea is Ireland's favourite drink, so it should come as no surprise that we also use it in our baking. Soaking the dried fruit in tea makes this cake very moist.

INGREDIENTS

225 ml/8 fl oz cold tea
200 g/7 oz sugar
175 g/6 oz mixed dried fruit
1 tsp mixed spice
1 tsp ground cinnamon
25 g/1 oz butter, plus extra for greasing and serving
250 g/9 oz self-raising flour
1 egg, beaten
butter, to serve

METHOD

Put the tea, sugar, dried fruit, mixed spice, cinnamon and butter into a saucepan and bring to the boil, stirring constantly, over a low heat. Remove from the heat and leave to cool.

Meanwhile, preheat the oven to 180°C/350°F/Gas Mark 4. Grease a 900-g/2-lb loaf tin with butter and line the base and sides with baking paper.

Add the flour and the egg to the cooled mixture and beat until well combined.

Pour the batter into the prepared loaf tin and bake in the preheated oven for 1 hour, or until a skewer inserted into the centre of the cake comes out clean. Cover with foil if the top is browning too quickly.

Leave to cool in the tin for 10 minutes, then turn out onto a wire rack to cool completely. Peel off the baking paper.

Slice thickly and serve with butter.

SERVES 8

GRANNY'S TIP: The cake will keep well for a few days in an airtight tin.

INGREDIENTS

150 g/5½ oz caster sugar

150 g/5½ oz butter, plus extra for greasing

3 eggs, lightly beaten

150 g/5½ oz self-raising flour

1½ tsp baking powder

½ tsp vanilla extract

icing sugar, for dusting

fresh berries, to decorate

Filling

4 tbsp home-made strawberry jam (page 226) or raspberry jam

250 ml/9 fl oz double cream, whipped

100 g/3½ oz fresh berries

SERVES 8

Victoria Sponge

This delicious cake can be a simple sponge sandwich with jam as a filling, but you can really push the boat out and add fresh cream and berries as well.

METHOD

Preheat the oven to 160°C/325°F/Gas Mark 3. Grease two 20-cm/8-inch sandwich tins with butter and line the bases with baking paper.

Beat the sugar and butter together until light and fluffy. Gradually add the eggs, alternating with two-thirds of the flour. Fold in the baking powder with the remaining flour and the vanilla extract.

Divide the batter between the prepared tins and bake in the preheated oven for 30 minutes. Leave to cool in the tins for 10 minutes, then turn out onto a wire rack to cool completely.

Spread the jam on the base of one of the cakes. Spread the cream on top, then scatter over the berries and top with the other cake. Decorate with berries, dust with icing sugar and serve immediately.

INGREDIENTS

175 g/6 oz treacle
55 g/2 oz golden syrup
100 g/3½ oz butter, plus extra for greasing
150 ml/5 fl oz milk
2 eggs, beaten
225 g/8 oz plain flour
55 g/2 oz caster sugar
2 tsp mixed spice
2 tsp ground ginger
1 tsp bicarbonate of soda
whipped cream, to serve

Ginger Cake

Treacle and golden syrup come together with a little sugar and spice to make this lusciously moist, dark ginger cake.

METHOD

Preheat the oven to 150°C/300°F/Gas Mark 2. Grease an 18-cm/7-inch square cake tin with butter and line the base with baking paper.

Put the treacle, golden syrup and butter into a saucepan and heat over a medium heat until the butter is melted. Add the milk and the eggs.

Sift the flour, sugar, spices and bicarbonate of soda together into a bowl. Add the treacle mixture and beat until smooth.

Pour the batter into the prepared tin and bake in the preheated oven for 1¼–1½ hours, or until a skewer inserted into the centre of the cake comes out clean.

Leave to cool in the tin for 10 minutes, then turn out onto a wire rack and leave to cool completely. Cut into squares and serve with whipped cream.

SERVES 6–9

INGREDIENTS

175 g/6 oz butter, softened, plus extra for greasing

175 g/6 oz caster sugar

175 g/6 oz self-raising flour, sifted

4 eggs, beaten

finely grated zest of 3 lemons

3 tsp lemon extract

Lemon Cake

This tangy lemon cake is delicious served with coffee or tea, or with whipped cream or ice cream as a dessert.

METHOD

Preheat the oven to 180°C/350°F/Gas Mark 4. Grease a small loaf tin or a 23-cm/9-inch round springform cake tin with butter and line with baking paper.

Cream the butter and sugar together until light and fluffy. Gradually add the flour and the eggs alternately, beating after each addition until incorporated.

Add the lemon zest and lemon extract, stirring well to combine. The batter will be quite stiff.

Transfer the batter to the prepared tin and bake in the preheated oven for 20 minutes. Reduce the oven temperature to 160°C/300°F/Gas Mark 2 and bake for a further 20–30 minutes, or until a skewer inserted into the centre of the cake comes out clean.

Leave to cool in the tin for 10 minutes, then unclip and remove the springform and leave to cool completely.

GRANNY'S TIP: If you don't have any lemon extract, you can add the juice of 3 lemons instead, but this will make a denser, heavier cake.

SERVES 8

INGREDIENTS

240 g/8½ oz butter, softened, plus extra for greasing

240 g/8½ oz caster sugar

4 large eggs, beaten

30 g/1 oz caraway seeds

½ tsp ground mace

½ tsp freshly ground nutmeg

325 g/11½ oz self-raising flour

3 tbsp brandy

4–6 tbsp milk

soft light brown sugar, for sprinkling

SERVES 6–8

Seed Cake

A good cake for visitors, traditionally served on Sundays. The caraway seeds add a sophisticated flavour, usually unpalatable to children but loved by adults.

METHOD

Preheat the oven to 180°C/350°F/Gas Mark 4. Grease an 18-cm/7-inch round cake tin with butter and line the base with baking paper.

Cream the butter and caster sugar together in a large bowl until pale and fluffy, then gradually add the eggs, beating after each addition until incorporated.

Add the caraway seeds, mace and nutmeg, then sift in the flour and fold it in. Stir in the brandy.

Add enough milk to loosen the batter to a good dropping consistency. Spoon the batter into the prepared tin, smoothing the surface with the back of a spoon. Sprinkle the brown sugar over the top.

Bake in the centre of the preheated oven for 40–50 minutes, or until a skewer inserted into the centre of the cake comes out clean. Leave to cool in the tin for 10 minutes, then turn out onto a wire rack to cool completely.

GRANNY'S TIP: The cake will taste even better after a day or two. Wrap it in foil and store it in an airtight tin for up to 5 days.

INGREDIENTS

500 g/1 lb 2 oz
Bramley apples,
peeled, cored and
cut into chunks

2 tbsp soft light
brown sugar

250 g/9 oz plain
flour, plus extra if
needed

½ tsp baking powder

100 g/3½ oz chilled
butter, plus extra for
greasing

100 g/3½ oz caster
sugar, plus extra for
dusting

1 large egg, beaten

100 ml/3½ fl oz
milk

flaked almonds, to
decorate

SERVES 8

Apple Cake

This cake is a cross between an apple tart and an apple pie. The texture of the pastry – a bit like a soft shortbread – is key.

METHOD

Preheat the oven to 180°C/350°F/Gas Mark 4. Grease a 20-cm/ 8-inch round loose-based cake tin with butter and line the base with baking paper.

Toss the apples with the brown sugar. Sift the flour and baking powder together into a bowl and rub in the butter until you achieve a breadcrumb texture.

Add the sugar, mixing it in with a blunt knife, then add the egg. Add the milk very gradually until a soft dough forms. Add more flour if the mixture becomes too wet to handle.

Spread half the dough in the base of the prepared tin, pressing it in with your knuckles. Tip in the apples, then place the remaining dough on top. Sprinkle with flaked almonds, then bake in the preheated oven for 40 minutes, or until the dough is golden and the apples are tender). Leave to cool in the tin for about 10 minutes, then turn out, dust with caster sugar and serve.

GRANNY'S TIP: Don't worry if the apple chunks poke through the uncooked pastry – this is normal when using a very soft dough.

INGREDIENTS

175 g/6 oz self-
raising flour
125 g/4½ oz caster
sugar
125 g/4½ oz butter,
softened
2 eggs, beaten
2 tbsp water
1 tsp vanilla extract
200 g/7 oz icing
sugar
2 tbsp lukewarm
water
sugar sprinkles, to
decorate

Queen Cakes

Children love to help with baking and
decorating these little cakes. They're very
popular for afternoon tea and, of course,
children's parties.

METHOD

Preheat the oven to 200°C/400°F/Gas Mark 6. Line two 8-hole
bun tins with paper cases.

Put the flour, caster sugar, butter, eggs, water and vanilla extract
into a bowl and beat until smooth. Fill the paper cases two-
thirds full with the batter.

Bake in the preheated oven for about 15 minutes until golden,
then transfer to a wire tray to cool completely.

Sift the icing sugar into a bowl and mix in enough of the
lukewarm water to make a thick, smooth paste. Spread the icing
over the cakes and scatter over some sprinkles. Leave to set,
then serve.

MAKES 16

*GRANNY'S TIP: If you'd prefer a coloured icing, just add a few drops of
liquid food colouring to the icing and stir well before spreading.*

INGREDIENTS

175 g/6 oz self-
raising flour
125 g/4½ oz caster
sugar
125 g/4½ oz butter
2 eggs, beaten
2 tbsp cold water
1 tsp vanilla extract
5 tbsp home-made
strawberry jam
(page 226) or
raspberry jam
5 tbsp whipped
cream
icing sugar, for
dusting

Butterfly Cakes

These impressive-looking cakes are
incredibly easy to make and very popular
as a tea-time treat.

METHOD

Preheat the oven to 200°C/400°F/Gas Mark 6. Line two 8-hole
bun tins with paper cases.

Put the flour, caster sugar, butter, eggs, cold water and vanilla
extract into a bowl and beat until smooth. Fill the paper cases
two-thirds full with the batter.

Bake in the preheated oven for about 15 minutes until golden,
then transfer to a wire tray to cool completely.

Cut the tops off the cakes and set aside. Put a teaspoon of jam
and a teaspoon of cream on top of each cake, then cut the
reserved pieces in half and place 2 halves on each cake, set at an
angle to imitate wings.

Dust with icing sugar just before serving.

MAKES 16

INGREDIENTS
350 g/12 oz rolled oats

175 g/6 oz demerara sugar

pinch of salt

225 g/8 oz butter, plus extra for greasing

2 tbsp golden syrup

Flapjacks

Also known as 'scrunch' in some parts of the country, these are a great favourite with children. They will keep in an airtight tin for a week or two – if you can keep them hidden from little fingers.

METHOD

Preheat the oven to 180°C/325°F/Gas Mark 4. Grease a baking tray with butter.

Put the oats, sugar and salt into a bowl and mix to combine.

Put the butter and golden syrup into a saucepan and heat over a medium heat until the butter is melted.

Pour the butter mixture over the dry ingredients and mix well. Press the mixture into the prepared tray, then bake in the preheated oven for 30 minutes.

Leave to cool in the tray for about 10 minutes, then cut into squares and transfer to a wire rack to cool completely.

MAKES
ABOUT 24

Oat & Honey Crunch Biscuits

These crunchy, slightly chewy biscuits are perfect for eating with your morning coffee. Add a handful of raisins or chocolate chips for a little touch of luxury.

INGREDIENTS

225 g/8 oz butter, plus extra for greasing

225 g/8 oz caster sugar

2 tsp clear honey

4 tbsp hot water

225 g/8 oz rolled oats

225 g/8 oz plain flour

1 tsp baking powder

1 tsp bicarbonate of soda

SERVES 4

METHOD

Preheat the oven to 190°C/375°F/Gas Mark 5 and grease two large baking sheets with butter.

Cream the butter and sugar together until soft and creamy. Add the honey and water and stir to combine.

Add the oats and sift in the flour, baking powder and bicarbonate of soda.

Mix well, then roll dessert spoons of the mixture into balls with your hands and flatten them on the prepared baking sheets, spaced well apart to allow for spreading during cooking.

Bake in the preheated oven for 10–15 minutes. Leave to cool on the baking sheets for 10 minutes, then use a spatula to transfer to wire racks to cool completely.

The biscuits can be stored in an airtight tin for up to 1 week.

GRANNY'S TIP: Wet your hands slightly before rolling the mixture into balls – this will prevent it sticking to your hands and you will be able to roll it more evenly.

PRESERVES & DRINKS

When you need a little something to
sweeten your scones or liven up your day,
Granny's lovely collection of jams, preserves
and drinks will hit the spot.

An rud nach leigheasann im ná uisce
beatha níl aon leigheas air.
What butter or whiskey does not
cure cannot be cured.

Irish Saying

Gooseberry Jam

This delicious, fresh-tasting jam made with just-ripe gooseberries is worlds away from the commercially produced variety.

INGREDIENTS

1.5 kg/3 lb 5 oz green gooseberries, topped and tailed
500 ml/18 fl oz water
1.5 kg/3 lb 5 oz preserving sugar
juice of 1 lemon

METHOD

Put the gooseberries into a preserving pan with the water and heat over a medium heat until simmering. Simmer for 30 minutes until the gooseberries are soft and the liquid has reduced by about a third.

Add the sugar and lemon juice and heat, stirring, until the sugar has dissolved. Bring to the boil and cook at a rapid boil for 10 minutes until the setting point has been reached (110°C/220°F).

Pour into sterilised jars and cover tightly.

MAKES 1 KG/
2 LB 4 OZ

GRANNY'S TIP: If you don't have a jam thermometer you can check for setting by putting a teaspoon of the hot jam onto a chilled saucer. If it wrinkles when you push your finger into it, the jam will set.

INGREDIENTS
1.5 kg/3 lb 5 oz
hulled strawberries
1.5 kg/3 lb 5 oz
preserving sugar
juice of 4 lemons

Strawberry Jam

This is probably everyone's favourite jam. Although strawberries can be expensive to buy, a lot of producers have 'pick-your-own' days, when you can pick a lot and pay very little.

METHOD

Layer the strawberries with the sugar in a large bowl and leave to stand overnight in a cool place.

Transfer to a preserving pan, add the lemon juice and bring to the boil over a very low heat, stirring constantly.

Cook at a rapid boil for 30 minutes, skimming off the foam occasionally, then test for setting (page 224).

When the setting point (110°C/220°F) has been reached, leave to cool in the pan for about 15 minutes, then pour into sterilised jars and cover tightly.

**MAKES 1 KG/
2 LB 4 OZ**

GRANNY'S TIP: Strawberries have very little pectin, so lemon juice is added to encourage the jam to set.

INGREDIENTS

1.8 kg/4 lb
blackberries
425 ml/15 fl oz
water
juice of 2-3 lemons
1 kg/2 lb 4 oz
preserving sugar

Bramble Jelly

There are many uses for blackberries,
but this tangy, gleaming jelly is one of
the most delicious. Blackberries have
no pectin content, so the lemon juice is
essential as a setting agent.

METHOD

Put the blackberries into a preserving pan with the water and
lemon juice and heat over a medium heat until simmering.
Simmer for about 30 minutes until the fruit is tender.

Mash the fruit, then pour into a jelly bag and leave to strain
overnight.

Return the liquid to the pan, add the sugar and heat over a
medium heat until dissolved. Bring to the boil and boil rapidly
for about 10 minutes, skimming off the foam occasionally, then
check for setting (page 224).

When the setting point (110°C/220°F) has been reached, pour
into sterilised jars and cover tightly.

**MAKES 1.3 KG/
3 LB**

*GRANNY'S TIP: Resist the temptation to press the juice through the jelly
bag – this will result in a cloudy jelly. If you don't have a jelly bag, line a
sieve with muslin and use that instead.*

INGREDIENTS

1 kg/2 lb 4 oz
Seville oranges
2.3 litres/4 pints
water
grated rind and juice
of 2 lemons
2 kg/4 lb 8 oz
preserving sugar
2 tbsp whiskey

Seville Orange Marmalade

Making a delicious marmalade can really cheer you up in the middle of a dreary January, when the bitter oranges from Seville are in season.

METHOD

Cut the oranges in half and squeeze the juice. Cut out the loose membrane, retaining the pith. Place the membrane in a muslin bag with the pips and soak in the cold water for 1 hour.

Chop the peel finely or thickly, to taste, then put into a large non-metallic bowl with the water, orange juice, lemon zest and juice, and the bag of pips. Leave to soak overnight.

Transfer the mixture to a large saucepan, bring to the boil, then reduce the heat and simmer for 2 hours, or until the peel is soft and the liquid has reduced by at least 50 per cent.

Add the sugar and stir to dissolve, then increase the heat, bring to a rolling boil and cook for about 5–10 minutes until the setting point is reached (110°C/220°F).

Add the whiskey, then pour into sterilised jars and cover tightly.

MAKES 3.2 KG/
7 LB

INGREDIENTS

1 kg/2 lb 4 oz
rhubarb, trimmed
and chopped into
2.5-cm/1-inch
lengths
1 kg/2 lb 4 oz
preserving sugar
juice of 2 lemons
2.5-cm/1-inch piece
fresh ginger

Rhubarb & Ginger Jam

Ginger is the perfect complement to rhubarb, and this jam makes good use of a seasonal glut of the fruit. The lemon juice, added for pectin content, gives a little extra zing.

METHOD

Put the rhubarb into a large bowl with the sugar, stir to combine, then leave to soak overnight.

Put the rhubarb into a non-aluminium preserving pan and add the lemon juice. Peel the ginger and grate it into the mixture.

Bring to the boil over a medium heat, then reduce the heat and simmer for about 20 minutes until the rhubarb is very soft and the liquid is syrupy.

Pour into sterilised jars and cover tightly.

MAKES ABOUT
1.8 KG/4 LB

INGREDIENTS

100 g/3½ oz butter
175 g/6 oz caster
sugar
finely grated zest
and juice of 2 large
lemons
3 large eggs, beaten

Lemon Curd

**Delicious in its own right as a spread, this
tangy preserve is also useful as a standby
ingredient for a range of cakes and tarts.**

METHOD

Put the butter, sugar and lemon zest and juice into a heatproof
bowl set over a saucepan of simmering water. Stir until the
butter has melted.

Add the eggs and stir for 20 minutes, or until the mixture has
thickened.

Pour into sterilised jars and cover tightly when cold.

**MAKES 450 G/
1 LB**

*GRANNY'S TIP: Lemon curd will keep for 1–2 weeks in a cool dark place,
but it doesn't have the shelf-life of most other preserves, so always make it
in small quantities.*

INGREDIENTS

1.4 kg/3 lb Bramley
apples, peeled,
cored and chopped

3 onions, chopped

1 litre/1½ pints
cider vinegar

900 g/2 lb soft light
brown sugar

½ tsp cayenne
pepper

2 tsp salt

350 g/12 oz
sultanas or raisins

pinch of mixed spice
or ground cloves

1 tbsp English
mustard powder

Apple Chutney

A good way of using up a glut of apples,
this chutney will enhance a whole range of
dishes, from cheese platters to curries.

METHOD

Put the apples and onions into a saucepan with the vinegar.
Bring to the boil over a medium heat, then reduce the heat and
simmer for about 20 minutes.

Add the remaining ingredients and mix well to combine. Return
to the boil, then reduce the heat and simmer for about 35
minutes, stirring occasionally to prevent sticking.

When the mixture is dark and thick spoon it into sterilised jars
and cover tightly.

MAKES 2.25 KG/
5 LB

INGREDIENTS

1 onion, finely
chopped

300 g/10½ oz fresh
pork mince

55 g/2 oz fresh
white breadcrumbs

1 tbsp chopped fresh
sage

1 tbsp chopped fresh
thyme

1 goose, about 6
kg/13 lb

350 ml/12 fl oz
chicken or goose
giblet stock

200 ml/7 fl oz red
wine

salt and freshly
ground black pepper

roast potatoes (page
116), to serve

SERVES 8–10

Roast Goose with Stuffing

Goose is back in fashion for Christmas
dinner. Make sure you get one that is large
enough for your crowd – goose loses a lot
of its fat and weight during roasting.

METHOD

Preheat the oven to 220°C/425°/Gas Mark 7. Mix the onion,
pork, breadcrumbs and herbs together and season to taste with
salt and pepper.

Put the stuffing into the neck flap end of the goose, securing
the flap with a skewer. Season the skin with salt and pepper,
then place the goose on a rack in a roasting tin and roast in the
preheated oven for 30 minutes.

Reduce the oven temperature to 180°C/350°F/Gas Mark 4 and
roast for a further 3½ hours, basting occasionally with the
cooking juices. Pierce the thickest part of the leg with a skewer;
if the juices run clear, the goose is cooked. Remove from the
oven and leave to rest for 20–30 minutes before serving.

Drain the fat from the tin, then place the tin over a low heat,
add the stock and wine and heat, stirring, to make a gravy.

Serve the goose with the gravy, stuffing and roast potatoes.

INGREDIENTS

1.3–1.8 kg/3–4 lb
spiced beef

600 ml/1 pint Irish
stout

1 onion, sliced

1 carrot, sliced

2 celery sticks, finely
sliced

1 small white turnip,
finely chopped

1 tsp ground allspice

Spiced Beef Marinated in Stout

Traditionally served cold on St Stephen's Day, spiced beef was a staple of the Irish Christmas. The stout marinade makes it very tender.

METHOD

Put the beef into a large bowl with the stout. Add enough water to cover and leave to marinate for 24 hours.

Remove the meat from the bowl and place in a large saucepan with the onion, carrot, celery, turnip and allspice. Cover with cold water, bring to the boil, then simmer for about 1 hour. Drain and discard the vegetables.

Meanwhile, preheat the oven to 180°C/350°F/Gas Mark 4. Transfer the beef to a roasting tin and cook in the preheated oven for 30 minutes.

Leave to cool completely. Slice thinly to serve.

SERVES 6–8

INGREDIENTS

250 g/9 oz currants
250 g/9 oz sultanas
or raisins
3 tbsp dark rum
250 ml/9 fl oz stout
butter, for greasing
100 g/3½ oz soft
dark brown sugar
60 g/2¼ oz plain
flour
1 tsp ground
cinnamon
1 tsp ground ginger
1 tsp mixed spice
1 large egg, beaten
55 g/2 oz fresh
white breadcrumbs

Rum butter

85 g/3 oz butter,
softened
85 g/3 oz demerara
sugar
5 tbsp dark rum

SERVES 12

Christmas Pudding with Rum Butter

Rum butter was a cheaper alternative to brandy butter, but its smoothness is a good complement to the pudding.

METHOD

Put the currants, sultanas, rum and stout into a large, non-metallic bowl, cover and leave overnight.

Grease a 1-litre/1¾-pint pudding basin. Cut out a 25-cm/10-inch square of foil and a 25-cm/10-inch square of baking paper, place together and pleat along the centre.

Add the remaining ingredients to the soaked fruit, stir well, then transfer to the prepared basin and level the surface. Place the pleated square on top, foil side up, then secure with string under the lip of the basin, finishing with a carrying loop.

Put the basin into a deep saucepan. Fill with water to halfway up the side of the basin. Cover tightly, bring to the boil, then reduce the heat and simmer for about 4½ hours, topping up the water as needed. Remove from the pan and leave to cool.

Wrap the basin in clingfilm. Store in a cool, dark place for up to 2 months. Reheat in a saucepan of simmering water for 2 hours.

To make the rum butter, cream the butter and sugar until light and fluffy. Beat in the rum very gradually, beating well after each addition until combined. Chill until ready to serve.

INGREDIENTS

500 g/1 lb 2 oz
ready-made trifle
sponges
150 ml/5 fl oz
medium sherry
250 g/9 oz raspberry
jam
600 ml/1 pint
whipped cream
flaked almonds, to
decorate

Creamy vanilla custard

600 ml/1 pint
double cream
4 large egg yolks
1 tbsp caster sugar
1 tsp vanilla extract

SERVES 8–10

Christmas Trifle

A traditional alternative to the Christmas pudding, made without the fresh or frozen fruit that is so often used nowadays. Serve in a cut-glass bowl, if you have one.

METHOD

Put the trifle sponges in the base of a large glass bowl and pour over the sherry. When it has soaked in, add the jam, spreading evenly.

To make the custard, heat the double cream in a large saucepan over a medium heat until hot but not boiling. Meanwhile, whisk the egg yolks, sugar and vanilla extract together in a bowl, then gradually pour in the hot cream and whisk to combine.

Transfer to a clean saucepan and heat over a low heat, whisking constantly, until the custard has thickened. Do not allow it to boil. If it starts to curdle, remove from the heat and place in a basin of cold water, whisking constantly.

Pour the custard over the jam and leave to chill overnight. Just before serving, spread the whipped cream over the top of the trifle and sprinkle with the flaked almonds.

GRANNY'S TIP: Use the best quality sherry you can – cooking sherry has no place in this recipe.

INGREDIENTS

600 ml/1 pint
double cream

1 tbsp caster sugar

zest of 1 lemon

1 tbsp lemon juice

200 ml/7 fl oz white
wine

100 g/3½ oz icing
sugar

½ tsp ground
cinnamon

freshly grated
nutmeg, for
sprinkling

boudoir biscuits, to
serve

SERVES 6

Christmas Syllabub

A really light and fresh alternative to Christmas pudding after an enormous Christmas dinner.

METHOD

Put the cream, caster sugar, lemon zest and lemon juice into a bowl and beat with a handheld electric mixer for 1 minute. Gradually add the wine and icing sugar, a third at a time, beating well after each addition.

Add the cinnamon and continue to beat until the cream holds soft peaks. Divide between 6 glasses and chill overnight.

Sprinkle with nutmeg and serve with boudoir biscuits.

For permission to reproduce copyright photographs, the publisher gratefully acknowledges the following:

background pattern Marina Mikhaylovich / Photos.com
p1 Ben Potter
p3 Laura Adamache / Shutterstock
p4 PierreLeclerc / Shutterstock
p 6 StephenLavery / Shutterstock
p12 Olga Miltsova / Shutterstock
p13 Dream79 / Shutterstock
p16 Jayme Burrows / Shutterstock
p17 Joerg Beuge / Laura Adamache / Shutterstock
p18 Robyn Mackenzie / Shutterstock
p20 Farbled / Shutterstock
p25 Walsh Photos / Shutterstock
p27 Margaret Edwards / Shutterstock
p29 Julie Deshaies / Shutterstock
p31 Ingrid Heczko / Shutterstock
p33 Egidijus Skiparis / Shutterstock
p35 Lilyana Vynogradova / Shutterstock
p37 Sea Wave / Shutterstock
p39 IngridHS / Shutterstock
p41 Saddako / Shutterstock
p43 Joe Gough / Shutterstock
p45 Travellight / Shutterstock
p47 Ben Potter
p49 Praisaeng / Shutterstock
p51 Ben Potter
p53 Yana Gayvoronskaya / Shutterstock
p55 Martin Turzak / Shutterstock
p57 Mathieu Boivin / Shutterstock
p59 Runin / Shutterstock
p61 Marmo81 / Shutterstock
p63 Ben Potter
p65 Magdanatka / Shutterstock

p67 Julietphotography / Shutterstock
p69 Ben Potter
p71 Ronald Sumners / Shutterstock
p73 Paul Cowan / Shutterstock
p75 Joe Gough / Shutterstock
p77 Kesu / Shutterstock
p79 Elzbieta Sekowska / Shutterstock
p81 Ben Potter
p83 Ablestock.com
p85 Magdanatka / Shutterstock
p87 Farbled / Shutterstock
p89 Tatiana Frank / Shutterstock
p91 Ampol Southong
p93 Ben Potter
p95 Atelier Joly
p97 Robyn Mackenzie / Shutterstock
p99 Ben Potter
p101 Jacek Chabraszewski / Shutterstock
p103 Bonchan / Shutterstock
p105 Ben Potter
p107 Lilyana Vynogradova / Shutterstock
p109 Kitch Bain / shutterstock
p111 Monkey Business Image / Shutterstock
p113 Ben Potter
p115 Bob Ingelhar / Shutterstock
p117 Paul Brighton / Shutterstock
p119 Kab Visio / Shutterstock
p121 Shtukicrew / Shutterstock
p123 Robyn Mackenzie / Shutterstock
p125 Ben Potter
p127 Neil Langan / Shutterstock
p129 Travellight / Shutterstock
p131 Ben Potter

p133 Ben Potter
p135 Ben Potter
p137 C Gissemann / Shutterstock
p139 Douglas Freer / Shutterstock
p141 Ben Potter
p143 Ekaterina Glazova / Shutterstock
p145 Joyce Marrero / Shutterstock
p147 Ben Potter
p149 Olyina / Shutterstock
p151 Ben Potter
p153 Ben Potter
p155 Irish Food Photo
p157 Isantilli / Shutterstock
p159 Ben Potter
p161 Travellight / Shutterstock
p163 Barbro Bergfeldt / Shutterstock
p165 Ben Potter
p167 Ben Potter
p169 Ben Potter
p171 Monkey Business Images / Shutterstock
p173 Bernashafo / Shutterstock
p175 Ildi Papp / Shutterstock
p177 Ben Potter
p179 Monkey Business Images / Shutterstock
p181 Walshphotos / Shutterstock
p183 Laura Adamache / Shutterstock
p185 Leigh Boardman / Shutterstock
p187 Lucie RÂhovÁ¡ / Shutterstock
p189 Ben Potter
p191 Robyn Mackenzie / Shutterstock
p193 Ben Potter
p195 Mrsiraphol / Shutterstock

p197 Gina Moore / Shutterstock
p199 Ben Potter
p201 Ben Potter
p203 ra3n / Shutterstock
p205 Magdanatka / Shutterstock
p207 Ben Potter
p209 R Conli / Shutterstock
p211 Ben Potter
p213 Magdanatka / Shutterstock
p215 Joerg Beuge / Shutterstock
p217 Monkey Business Images / Shutterstock
p219 Anthony Buckingham / Shutterstock
p221 Ben Potter
p223 Anthony Ricci / Shutterstock
p225 Christian Jung / Shutterstock
p227 Christian Jung / Shutterstock
p229 de2marco / Shutterstock
p231 Oxana Denezhkina / Shutterstock
p233 Christian Jung / Shutterstock
p235 Elena Shashkina / Shutterstock
p237 Ksena2you / Shutterstock
p239 Olga Miltsova / Shutterstock
p241 Wollertz / Shutterstock
p243 Ben Potter
p245 Gerardo Borbolla / Shutterstock
p247 Shebeko / Shutterstock
p249 Anna Hoychuk / Shutterstock
p251 Monkey Business Images / Shutterstock
p253 Ben Potter
p255 Ben Potter